The 'West', Islam and Islamism

The 'West', Islam and Islamism

Is ideological Islam compatible with liberal democracy?

Caroline Cox
and
John Marks

Civitas: Institute for the Study of Civil Society
London

First published June 2003
Civitas
The Mezzanine, Elizabeth House
39 York Road, London SE1 7NQ
email: books@civitas.org.uk

ISBN 1-903 386-29 2

Typeset by Civitas
in New Century Schoolbook

Printed in Great Britain by
The Cromwell Press
Trowbridge, Wiltshire

Contents

Authors

Caroline Cox was created a Life Peer in 1982 and has been a deputy speaker of the House of Lords since 1985. She was Founder Chancellor of Bournemouth University, 1991-2001; and is a Vice President of the Royal College of Nursing. She is heavily involved with international humanitarian and human rights work, serving as a non-executive director of the Andrei Sakharov Foundation; as a Trustee of MERLIN (Medical Emergency Relief International) and the Siberian Medical University; Honorary President of Christian Solidarity Worldwide-UK; and Chairman of the Executive Board of the International Islamic Christian Organisation for Reconciliation and Reconstruction (IICORR).

Lady Cox has been honoured with the Commander Cross of the Order of Merit of the Republic of Poland and the Wilberforce Award for her humanitarian work. She has also been awarded an Honorary Fellowship of the Royal College of Surgeons of England and honorary doctorates by universities in the United Kingdom, the United States of America, the Russian Federation, and Armenia.

Baroness Cox's work in the field of humanitarian aid and human rights has taken her on many missions to conflict zones including the Armenian enclave of Nagorno Karabackh; many missions to Sudan; to be with the Karen and Karenni people in the jungles of Eastern Burma; and with communities suffering from religious conflict in Indonesia.

John Marks is director of the Civitas Education Unit and co-director, with Baroness Cox, of the Educational Research Trust. He was formerly administrator of the National Council for Educational Standards (NCES) and has over 40 years of teaching experience in universities, polytechnics and schools. He was a member of the Schools Examination and Assessment Council, 1990-3, the National Curriculum Council, 1992-3, and Schools Curriculum and Assessment Authority, 1993-7. He is currently vice chairman of the governors of a comprehensive school, having first been elected as a parent governor in 1978. His many publications on education include: *Standards in Schools: Assessment, Accountability and the Purpose of Education* (The Social Market Foundation, 1991); *Value for Money in Education: Opportunity Costs and the Relationship between Standards and Resources* (Campaign for Real Education, 1992); *Vocational Education, Training and Qualifications in Britain* (IEA, 1996); *Standards of English and Maths in Primary Schools for 1995* (Social Market Foundation, 1996); *Standards of Arithmetic: How to Correct the Decline* (Centre for Policy Studies, 1996); *Standards of Reading, Spelling and Maths for 7-year-olds in Primary Schools for 1995* (Social Market Foundation, 1997); *A Selective or Comprehensive System: Which Works Best? The Empirical Evidence* (Centre for Policy Studies, 1998); *An Anatomy of Failure: Standards in English Schools for 1997* (Social Market Foundation, 1998); *Value for Money in LEA Schools* (Centre for Policy Studies, 1998); *What are Special Educational Needs? An Analysis of a New Growth Industry* (Centre for Policy Studies, 2000); *The Betrayed Generations: Standards in British Schools 1950-2000* (Centre for Policy Studies, 2001) and *Girls Know Better: Educational Attainment of Boys and Girls* (Civitas, 2001). He is also the author of *Fried Snowballs: Communism in Theory and Practice* (Claridge Press, 1990).

Foreword

The aim of this book is to encourage reconciliation and mutual understanding between Islam and the West. As the authors acknowledge, to speak of the West is not to describe a uniform tradition of thought. The West has been torn between authoritarianism and democracy and between totalitarianism and liberalism. There were times during the last century when the triumph of democracy and liberalism were by no means certain. And, if we go back further still in Western history, Christianity itself was bitterly divided in the sixteenth and seventeenth centuries between Catholic and Protestant.

However, if Lord Acton is to be believed, this conflict taught people 'to treasure the liberties of others as their own, and to defend them for love of justice and charity more than as a claim of right'.[1] In political terms, our ancestors learnt that it was only by limiting the powers of government that religious freedom could be assured. The bargain was that all religious sects agreed to abide by the law of the land, on the understanding that none would try to use the powers of the state to persecute opponents or to punish members of their own faith who wished to leave. Once this basic loyalty to the nation was accepted, people of all faiths were free to lead their lives according to the ideals they cherished most.

If there was an underlying belief, it was that human reason and self-restraint were fragile things. For this reason, no one should be trusted with too much power, particularly those who thought they had a divine right to rule or who believed that their opinions were derived from sacred and unchanging precepts. Instead, liberalism put its faith, not in relativism—which is a corruption of the idea that human reason is fallible—but in the belief that we could get closer to the truth through a process of mutual learning by means of public discussion and openness to contradiction. This ideal required religions to tolerate criticism in the hope that they might learn from their opponents. And it meant that no one should claim that it was an 'insult' to question their fundamental beliefs. For liberals, all beliefs must remain open to challenge. There is a tendency among some Muslim leaders to accuse any critic of Islam of 'Islamophobia'. This attitude makes no distinction between legitimate criticism of Islam and sheer prejudice. In a liberal society we must all learn to be thick-skinned, lest our sensitivities prevent us from facing up to the truth.

Islamism, the name the authors and other authorities give to Islamic fundamentalism, is the exact opposite of Western liberal-democracy. It is a brand of totalitarianism rooted in a sacred text—the very idea rejected in the seventeenth century after long years of bloodshed. By making a sharp distinction between Islamism and mainstream Islam the authors hope to avoid alienating moderate Muslims. But they do not duck delicate issues or tip-toe around substantive differences. Liberalism emerged precisely to create a political framework under which people who disagreed strongly could live in harmony.

One other sensitivity should be dealt with. The book quotes some writers who call for the reform of Islam. When fellow Muslims, such as Tariq Ali (pp. 73-74), have advocated change there has been resentment enough, but when non-Muslims raise questions about the nature of Islam, it can give rise to bitter hostility. It is, therefore, very important that any such questions are asked, not out of a complacent sense of Western superiority, but in the true spirit of liberal democracy. Moreover, to say as much is not a token concession. The West is successful economically and technologically, but Western culture is the subject of a hotly contested debate. High rates of crime and family breakdown, and the high level of anti-social behaviour have caused widespread concern. Britain is at the top end of European league for teenage pregnancy, youthful drunkenness and drug-taking. Many of our social affairs intelligentsia have spent the last 40 years denigrating Western achievements and undermining the principle of moral self-restraint on which liberal civilisation depends. Even the defenders of liberty have lost the confidence necessary to offer an inspiring social ideal for each successive generation to emulate.

The authors, therefore, do not write in a spirit of self-satisfied support for their own culture, but because they know that changing events present all cultures with the constant challenge of both renewing the best in their own heritage whilst also relaxing the hold of doctrines that no longer make sense.

In particular, it is our hope that this book will encourage a public debate about how best to avoid renewed religious conflict within a liberal constitutional framework that makes religious freedom possible.

David G. Green

1

Introduction:
A Comparison Between
'Western' and 'Islamic' World-Views

Definitions and distinctions

Since September 11, 2001, open almost any Western newspaper almost any day and you will find dramatic headlines describing 'The War Against Terrorism', highlighting Islamic or Islamist activities.

On that fateful morning, the 'West' woke up to the phenomenon of militant, violent Islamism, which had already been active in many other parts of the world, including the Philippines, Pakistan, Indonesia, Sudan and Nigeria as well as the Middle East.

But there is another aspect of Islam which has not featured so strongly in the media in the aftermath of September 11. There are over a billion Muslims in the world today. The vast majority of them lead law-abiding lives and live peaceably with their neighbours, including those of other faiths. In many countries and cultures, they are respected for their hospitality, generosity and graciousness.

Moreover, some nation states, such as Indonesia—the world's largest Islamic nation, with over 200 million people, the vast majority of whom are Muslim—have enshrined the principles of cultural pluralism and religious tolerance in their constitution. The words 'Unity in Diversity' are inscribed in Indonesia's national emblem.

But there is also cause for concern. In countries such as Nigeria and Sudan, relationships between Muslims and those of other faiths, such as Christians and traditional believers, have long been harmonious, with mutual respect, friendship and shared participation in community events, such as weddings. But recent years have seen the development of more violent movements, with bitter conflict, fighting, death and destruction. In Sudan, the toll of human suffering is the greatest in the world today. With over two million dead and over five million displaced, the scale of human misery exceeds that of Somalia, Rwanda and former Yugoslavia taken together.

It is therefore important to try to understand these developments. Those who have the privilege of living in freedom need to consider the implications of threats to freedom in their own societies and the suffering being inflicted on innocent victims elsewhere. Those who find themselves caught up in the conflicts in countries such as Sudan or Nigeria need to understand some of the forces at work in order to develop appropriate responses.

We also hope that this discussion will enhance mutual understanding between Muslims and non-Muslims and thereby help to develop harmonious relationships, based on an appreciation of shared values and insights into differences in their respective world-views.

This paper attempts to analyse some aspects of the current situation. It focuses on the philosophical and epistemological principles which underpin and shape the political and social institutions of 'Western' and 'Islamic' societies. We intend to publish a more detailed book-length study as soon as possible.[1]

The terms 'Western' and 'Islamic' represent very broad and heterogeneous categories. Any comparison will inevitably involve simplification but the following definitions and distinctions may be helpful.

1. Modern 'Western' societies base their philosophical principles, political institutions and social structures on the values of liberal democracy. These were historically rooted in Ancient Greece and developed by peoples influenced primarily by Judaeo-Christian traditions. The term 'Western' is now inappropriate geographically but we will use this nomenclature as it is widely used to refer to a constellation of societies which may differ from each other in many respects but which generally share fundamental philosophical, political and social characteristics. The defining characteristics of 'liberal democracy' include a commitment to fundamental freedoms, within a framework of laws designed to prevent their abuse, such as freedom to practice one's own religion; freedom of speech; freedom of association; freedom to publish; and equality before the law.

The populations of Western societies are very heterogeneous in many ways, including race, religion (or lack of religious commitment), culture, wealth and life-style. However, they are bound by the legal systems of the countries they inhabit and therefore committed to a respect for the associated values and their behavioural requirements.

Moreover, within the legal systems and political institutions, there are provisions for transparency and accountability. Although no system is fool-proof, there are institutionalised mechanisms for procedures to bring people and organisations to account. Therefore, despite the enormous heterogeneity between and within modern Western societies it is possible to indicate broadly defining characteristics which allow some generalisations.

It must also be acknowledged that there are recent examples of societies and individuals within the broad category Western societies which deviate from the central defining tenets of commitment to fundamental freedoms and the associated values of tolerance and respect for cultural diversity. The development of National Socialism in Nazi Germany is one such example. The religious and political intolerance of certain fundamentalist Christian groups, even towards other Christians, may offer examples at the level of individual beliefs and practices.

2. 'Islamic' societies. For many reasons modern 'Islamic' societies are more difficult to categorise. The term may be used to include a very heterogeneous range of societies, cultures and peoples.

For example, there are Islamic societies which have made explicit commitments to some of the values identified as those relating to Western societies. Many of these derive from a number of attempts to develop the concepts of traditional Islam to take account of the changes in Western societies which have led to modernisation. These include the emergence of 'modernist' Islam in the nineteenth and early twentieth centuries[2] and the related development of 'liberal' Islam mainly in the second half of the twentieth century.[3]

Practical consequences include the adoption of secular constitutions with commitments to secular legal systems and to the protection of individual freedoms, such as freedom of choice of religion, freedom of speech, publication and equality before the law.

Examples of societies with predominantly Muslim populations which have adopted such principles include Turkey in the 1920s, Indonesia after 1945, Egypt in the 1950s and Nigeria after independence in 1960.[4]

By contrast, there are societies where the ruling elites are committed to the maintenance of 'traditional' Islamic institutions and their associated values. These may have different manifestations. For example, Saudi Arabia maintains very strict adherence to *shari'a* law and many associated behavioural practices—curtailing freedoms such as the freedom of worship by adherents of other faiths or equality before the law between men and women, Muslims and non-Muslims.

Or there is the example of Sudan, which has suffered civil war for all but ten years since independence in 1956. One of the major causes of this bitter conflict has been the deep divisions between the beliefs and values among different sections of its diverse population. In 1989, the National Islamic Front (NIF) took power by military coup. It represents no more than about five per cent of the Sudanese people and those who oppose it include many Arab and African Muslims as well as many Christians and traditional believers. One of the primary causes of the opposition is the NIF's commitment to the imposition of *shari'a* law. Although the NIF argues that it will only apply to Muslims, many Muslims do not want this kind of legal system; and many Christians argue that it will impact on them, even if they are formally subject to a secular legal system.

Therefore, it is clear that the term 'Islamic societies' does not have the same broadly defining characteristics as the term Western societies and it is therefore very difficult to make generalisations referring to countries where the majority of citizens are Muslims. Any attempt to make such generalisations is also hampered by differences in the definition of the term 'Islam' and its relationship to the personal identity of its adherents. However, efforts have been made to make some definitions and distinctions. Given the complexity of the situation, these are inevitable over-simplifications, but may be helpful as a basis for analysis necessary to discuss and to try to understand historical developments and current situations.

We have found the definitions offered by Ruthven among the most helpful. He distinguishes between 'Islam' as identity, 'Islam' as faith, 'Islam as political ideology' and 'Islamism'.[5]

'Islam' as identity may refer to someone whose father is a Muslim and who accepts a nominal Muslim identity but without committing himself or herself to specifically Muslim beliefs and practices. Similarly in Western societies citizens may adopt, say, a nominal Christian or Jewish identity, without accepting any specifically Christian or Jewish commitments.

'Islam' as faith: 'Islam' is the Arabic word denoting submission or self-surrender to Allah as revealed through the message and life of his Prophet Mohammed. Many deeply committed Muslims may challenge the authenticity of 'nominal' or 'secular' Muslims.

'Islam' as political ideology may refer to the beliefs and practices of those Muslims who seek to establish an Islamic state in order to enforce obedience to the Islamic law or *shari'a* derived from the Koran and the life and sayings of the Prophet Mohammed. Methods vary according to different political situations. Jordan and Indonesia include some of those committed to this agenda among their parliamentarians at the heart of national government. By contrast, in Algeria they are in armed conflict with the state. In Sudan, the National Islamic Front régime took and maintains power by military force. In Nigeria, there are now eleven states imposing *shari'a* law in ways which have sometimes led to violent conflict with local Christian communities. Some Muslims claim that this process is part of an agenda to change the constitution and to transform Nigeria into an Islamic state.[6]

In some cases the supporters of 'political Islam' work within the framework of democratic institutions, using democracy and its enshrined freedoms in order, ultimately, to overthrow democracy and its associated freedoms and to replace them with their commitment to the sovereignty of God as expressed in the *shari'a*.[7]

'Islamism' and 'Islamist' are the terms now widely used to refer to radical, militantly ideological versions of Islam, as interpreted by the practitioners and in which violent actions such as terrorism, suicide bombings or revolutions are explicitly advocated, practised and justified using religious terminology. The Arabic prefix, which refers to the religion of 'Islam', is linked to the Latin suffix, indicating the politicisation of aspects of the religion. Similar mutations of words and concepts can be seen in 'communism', 'fascism', and 'socialism'. In all three cases, originally politically neutral words were thus given ideological meaning often suffused with implications for violent or revolutionary political action.

In general, the term 'Islamic societies' ranges from those with secular constitutions where a majority of citizens identify themselves as Muslims, as in Indonesia, to those where the ruling élites may adhere to a more political form of Islam or Islamism, as in Sudan. Saudi Arabia as the location of Mecca and Medina, the main Muslim holy places, is a special case.[8]

In our analysis, we will generally use the terms 'Islam' and 'Islamic societies', emphasising the caveat that it is a very broad, loose categorisation, encompassing a heterogeneous group of very different types of society and peoples with very different ways of life. We shall endeavour to highlight significant defining differences, as appropriate. We will refer to 'traditional Islam' to represent the development of Islamic doctrines from the seventh century up to approximately the ninth century. Islamists frequently refer to these doctrines in their writings and statements. It is therefore sometimes necessary to consider the tenets of traditional Islam in tandem with those of Islamists because this is what they themselves do.

Modernist and liberal Muslims—in countries in which Muslims are in a majority or a minority—have attempted to develop, adapt or reinterpret these traditional doctrines in the light of different situations over the period from the early nineteenth century up to the present.

We will maintain a distinction between the terms 'Islamic societies' and 'Islamism' because this represents the current *de facto* situation in which Islamist militant groups are adopting the traditional ideology and linking it with tactics of terrorism to pursue their agendas.

Prevention of the growth of Islamophobia

We believe that it is very important to emphasise this distinction, in order to prevent the development of Islamophobia. The vast majority of Muslims around the world are peaceable, law-abiding citizens. But there is a grave risk of a backlash against these peaceable Muslims in response to the terrorist activities of some Islamists. For terrorism breeds fear and fear breeds irrationality. Irrational fear does not make distinctions and therefore a hostile response to Islamist terrorism can quickly spread to hostility to all Muslims.

As we believe it is of the utmost importance to try to prevent this Islamophobia, it is our hope, and our intention in writing this book, that non-Muslims may develop a better understanding of aspects of Islam in order to develop more informed relationships with Muslims and appropriate responses to the current complex situation.

We write as non-Muslims who sincerely seek to promote peace and mutual respect between people of different faiths and cultures. One example of our commitment to this goal is an involvement in the establishment of the International Islamic Christian Organisation for Reconciliation and Reconstruction (IICORR). The former President of Indonesia, Abdurrhaman Wahid, has agreed to serve as its Honorary President and other distinguished Muslims and Christians are patrons. Its primary objective is to support the commitments and endeavours of peaceable 'moderate' Muslims and Christians caught up in intercommunal conflict to re-establish peace, to rebuild shattered lives and communities and to establish harmonious relationships.[9]

We also hope that our analysis and the questions it raises may assist Muslims to address these issues in ways which can enable them to help non-Muslims to understand Islam better. It is only through mutual understanding that respect can be promoted and provide a basis not only for peaceful co-existence but for mutually beneficial and enhancing relationships between two of the greatest belief-systems the world has known: modern 'liberal-democratic' 'Western societies' and the broad range of societies we can generally designate as 'Islamic societies'.

We are aware that much of our analysis may appear critical. However, it is not intended to be confrontational; it is derived from serious consideration of the issues involved and a genuine wish to understand the response of Muslims to them.

Given the heterogeneity of the 'Islamic world' and differences among those who identify themselves as Muslims we do not expect that there are single or simple answers to the questions we raise. But we hope they will not generate a hostile response, for we are not seeking to be adversarial, but to understand the Muslim point of view. We believe that many people in 'Western societies' share many of these concerns or the issues they reflect. It would therefore be a great help if they can be addressed in constructive dialogue.

One of the most urgent issues is the question of whether the distinction between Islam and Islamism is inherent; or whether peaceable Islam may be endangered by the beliefs and practices of radical Islamists, determined to impose their own agenda upon their co-religionists. This is perhaps the greatest challenge facing Islam today and one which is of inevitable concern to the rest of the world. If we have failed to make these or other necessary distinctions, we ask Muslims themselves to make the distinctions clear and thus to enable us and other non-Muslims to understand them.

Methodology: the use of 'Ideal Types' to compare 'Western' and 'Ideological' societies

The concept of 'Ideal Types' originally developed by Max Weber can be used to compare Western, traditional Islamic and Islamist societies.[10] These latter can be characterised by certain essential elements which allow their inclusion in the broader category of 'Ideological' societies.

The concept 'Ideal Type' refers to a constellation of characteristics generally associated with a particular category of social institutions. The components may vary significantly in detail, but share enough fundamental aspects to enable them to be classed together as a 'type' as a basis for comparison with other categories of social institutions.[11]

The principal ideological societies of the last century were those based on fascism—such as National Socialist Germany (1933-1945)—and those based on Marxist communism—such as the Soviet Union (1917-1991), its satellites in Eastern and Central Europe and its colonies such as Cuba or Mozambique; and communist China (1949-present). Both fascism and communism posed potentially lethal threats to Western societies. Nazi fascism was defeated after a six-year world war which cost millions of lives, including the six million Jews killed for ideological reasons in the death camps of the 1940s. The defeat of Marxism took longer and the casualties were greater—up to 60 million or more, according to the best estimates, including those killed in the myriad camps of the gulag in Siberia and elsewhere, again mostly for ideological reasons.[12]

But it was the long ideological battles of the Cold War and the massive efforts by Marxists to subvert, and thus to subdue, Western societies from within that was most difficult for the citizens of these societies to understand and thus effectively to resist.[13]

In this century, Islamism has emerged as a comparably dangerous threat to Western societies. Like the Marxists before them, Islamists are using the fundamental values and freedoms of Western societies to attack and to seek to destroy them. The main difference is that Islamists believe in what they are doing with a religious fervour that justifies mass murder and self-immolation, as we witness frequently in the Middle East and saw in New York on September 11, 2001. But virtually nobody in the latter-day Soviet Union or elsewhere believed in Marxism to the extent that they would commit suicide for the cause. This is one fundamental difference between Marxism and Islamism; the latter carries within its basic teachings a justification for martyrdom in the name of *jihad* or 'Holy War' even though suicide is explicitly forbidden in the Koran.

The suicide killings at the World Trade Centre and the Pentagon are examples of this phenomenon. The bombings were well planned, well financed and carried out with sophistication. Similarly, those carried out by teenagers during the Palestinian Intifada in Israel illustrate the religious justification and social support which motivate the suicide killers. They follow directly from the tenets of Islamism and are publicly justified as such in much of the media in many Islamic countries. They are organised, planned, ideologically justified and premeditated. They involve a massive investment of physical resources over many years and an education/propaganda programme that often starts with children as young as eight. In Palestinian summer camps children from eight to 12 begin the training that leads to some of them becoming suicide bombers.[14] They are systematically selected and trained. Their missions are planned and have institutional backing. Their martyrdom is subsequently celebrated and their families are given financial support.

> The bomber's family and the sponsoring organisation celebrate his martyrdom with festivities, as if it were a wedding. Hundreds of guests congregate at the house to offer congratulations. The hosts serve the juices and sweets that the young man specified in his will. Often, the mother will ululate in joy over the honour that Allah has bestowed upon her family.[15]

These suicide bombers are not described as such in much of the Islamic world—they are holy martyrs in an Islamic *jihad* or holy war and are therefore guaranteed direct admission to 'paradise' and all the honour due to such *jihad* martyrs (see section on *jihad* in Chapter 2).[16]

This book compares Western societies with ideological societies at two levels. The most fundamental level involves the concepts of knowledge and truth—how they are obtained and preserved and what kinds of values and institutions are needed for these purposes. Western societies and ideological societies give radically different answers to these epistemological questions. These differences in fundamental values and principles underpin, shape and give rise to very different social and political structures.

The purpose of our analysis is to seek to describe and document these differences in the hope that greater understanding may promote greater commitment to peaceful co-existence and mutual co-operation. Alternatively, in the undesirable event of mounting hostility, greater understanding of some of the fundamental differences may assist Western democratic societies to develop appropriate responses to challenges and threats to their survival. These threats now mainly concern militant Islam with its global claims and global reach because, since the early 1990s, a radical form of organised Islamism has proliferated and obtained the means to pursue its expansionist aims in many countries both within existing Islamic states and without.

2

Concepts of Knowledge and Truth

Epistemological principles: the academic mode and academies in 'Western' societies

The term 'mode' is used here to denote a system of values, principles and associated practices.

The core purpose of academies or universities in Western societies is to preserve, transmit and extend knowledge in ways which can be classified as 'the academic mode'. Academic procedures in such academies are based on the values of openness, tentativeness and pluralism. Criticism is welcomed as vital in the search for truth.

Criteria for the validation of knowledge derive from:

- the rules of logic and scientific inference;
- open discussion of alternatives;
- a commitment to attempts to refute and falsify currently held beliefs and practices;
- a commitment to test hypotheses with all the available relevant evidence.

Academic freedom is valued for both individuals and institutions provided they respect the academic authority of those who acknowledge, and help to institutionalise, the crucial criteria for the validation of knowledge.

Academies such as universities, colleges and research institutes seek, as much as is possible, to separate academic work from politics. The relative autonomy of the academies, their eschewal of emotional and moral pressure, and their relative freedom from political pressures are prized as necessary conditions for the pursuit of truth.

This academic mode is a way of thought and procedure which has been gradually articulated and established over the centuries in the academies of Western Europe and is one of the prime gifts of European civilisation to the world. It has led to the growth over the last three centuries of the vast body of scientific and technological knowledge which has transformed first Europe and then the rest of the world.

The growth of modern science

The rapid growth of modern science started about three hundred years ago in seventeenth century Europe. Since then science has built up a substantial body of knowledge —both about the world as it now is and about the history of man, the earth, the solar system and the universe.[1] In the twentieth century science has continued to grow rapidly and has ceased to be an activity of importance and interest only to experts. Because of modern science, technology and medicine, hundreds of millions of people are alive today who would previously have died in infancy or childhood.

If modern science, technology and medicine were to vanish from the world today, many hundreds of millions of people would die. The death toll from the loss of sources of energy, of mechanised and scientific agriculture and from the abandonment of scientific medicine and preventative health care would overshadow that from any previous period in world history. Modern science is indispensable for the survival of any future world society, no matter how it may evolve or be organised. But it also brings the potential for destruction on an unprecedented scale—either through purposeful destruction, with the use of biological, chemical or nuclear weapons, or through human error, as happened with the disaster at Chernobyl.

It is therefore important to understand how science develops and the criteria, values and institutions involved in establishing scientific knowledge.

Criteria and values

The criteria of logical coherence and the use of all available relevant evidence require a commitment to the fundamental values of open criticism, tentativeness and pluralism. These are involved in all kinds of academic enquiry but their effectiveness is enhanced by the special nature of science. The widespread use of mathematics forces scientists to make their concepts more precise and reveals more easily the logical implications of these concepts. And the evidence available to scientists from observation is greatly increased by the use of controlled and repeatable experiments. The testing of predictions by observation and controlled experiment, followed by the modification of concepts, if necessary, and further testing by experiment are the main mechanisms by which science has developed over the centuries. The process requires an essential humility in the search for truth: a willingness by scientists to subject their work to self-criticism and to criticism by other scientists.

Pluralism and tentativeness—the other key values—are associated with the need for public criticism and with the recognition that no individual or group can claim to have complete knowledge. The characteristics of the natural world and of human nature are far too complex to allow total and finite understanding.

The scholars of Ancient Greece such as Xenophanes (570-480 BC) recognised this:

> The gods did not reveal, from the beginning,
> All things to us, but in the course of time
> Through seeking we may learn and know things better.
> But as for certain truth, no man has known it...

Recent formulations include those by Karl Popper with his description of the essentially provisional nature of scientific knowledge in *Conjectures and Refutations* and his analysis of the need for tentativeness and gradual reform in the social sciences and social policy in *The Open Society and Its Enemies*.[2]

The latter work highlights the inherent dangers for freedom and quality of life when those in power believe they have a monopoly of truth and knowledge and seek to impose their versions of an ideal society on their citizens.

The academic mode also requires scientists to avoid using emotional arguments and moral and political pressures in

presenting their work. Recognition of the enormous problems involved in establishing knowledge means that, in
teaching, publishing and in research, academic practitioners should avoid any form of presentation which would
deflect attention from the logical coherence of claims to
knowledge and from the experimental evidence which
supports these claims.

The scientific community

The enormous body of scientific knowledge would not exist
without individual scientists who, in turn, could not operate
effectively without the institutions of the international
scientific community—scientific societies, scientific journals, academies of higher education, research organisations
and international conferences which are all in continual
interaction both with each other and with each individual
scientist operating according to the criteria and values
mentioned above. There are now tens of thousands of
learned scientific journals. By publishing their work in such
journals scientists expose their research to the public
scrutiny of their fellow experts. All the scientific work of
individuals is done in the knowledge that it will have to be
subjected to open public criticism by the scientific community and that it will stand or fall on the criteria of logic and
evidence. This is how the scientific community generates a
vastly greater stock of collectively validated knowledge than
any individual or centralised group could possibly do. It is
to safeguard this mode of operation that the scientific
community has to insulate itself from political and social
pressures.

The origins of the academic mode

This mode of operation of the scientific community had its
origins in Ancient Greece, was largely lost during the Dark
Ages of Western Europe and re-emerged in the medieval
European universities in the twelfth and thirteenth centuries, such as Bologna, Paris, Oxford and Cambridge. Other
academies soon developed and continued to do so over the
next eight hundred years.

Independent universities were possible in the Middle Ages because both the Christian church and the state recognised the independence of each other and of corporate entities like universities. The universities had the legal right to determine what and whom they taught, who should teach and the criteria for the degrees awarded. The curriculum was overwhelmingly composed of the exact sciences, logic, and natural philosophy. And it:

> ... was a permanent fixture for approximately 450 to 500 years. It was the curriculum of the arts faculty, which was the largest of the traditional four faculties of a typical major university, the others being medicine, theology, and law. Courses in logic, natural philosophy, geometry, and astronomy formed the core curriculum for the baccalaureate and master of arts degrees and were taught on a regular basis for centuries. These two arts degrees were virtual prerequisites for entry into the higher disciplines of law, medicine, and theology...[3]

Students of theology in the medieval European universities therefore began their main studies with considerable knowledge of logic and the sciences.[4]

This however did not prevent many examples of intellectual intolerance and religious bigotry in Western Europe over the centuries. These include the many conflicts during the Reformation and counter-reformation between those such as Copernicus and Galileo who sought some degree of academic and intellectual freedom on scientific and other matters and those in the Christian churches—both Catholic and Protestant—who resisted such changes using, on the Catholic side, instruments such as the Inquisition and the Index of Prohibited Books while amongst Protestant there were many fiercely antagonistic and intolerant sects.

Frequently these conflicts erupted into wars of religion between Christians of different persuasions in the sixteenth and seventeenth centuries. It took many years and many small steps before the current relatively tolerant compromise was reached. For example intolerance and separateness in educational institutions—including universities—persisted amongst Christians until well into the nineteenth and even, in some cases, into the twentieth centuries. Moreover the West was also slow to respect the equal rights of religious minorities such as Jews, agnostics and atheists.

Early Islamic achievements

For several centuries after the birth of Islam in 622 many aspects of academic endeavour and cultural creativity flourished in Islamic societies.

In particular, in eighth century Baghdad under the Abbasids many of the classic books of other cultures such as Ancient Greece, preserved by the Byzantines and Nestorians, and Ancient Persia were translated into Arabic and preserved over the next five hundred years in libraries over much of the Islamic world, which had rapidly expanded during the seventh and eighth centuries.

Over these centuries there were a number of outstanding Islamic contributions to the arts and sciences including the development of new knowledge in mathematics in the work of al-Hwarizmi (early ninth century) in algebra and al-Khayyam (d. 1123) on cubic equations; in observational astronomy with the development of a number of new instruments such as the quadrant and the astrolabe (ninth to thirteenth centuries) and the establishment of the famous observatory at Maraga; in optics with the pioneering work of al-Haytham (d. 1039); and in medicine with the work of Avicenna (d. 1037), whose *Canon* magisterially surveyed and encompassed both current knowledge and the knowledge of the Ancient World, and with, for example, the commissioning by caliph Abd-ur-Rahman (d. 961) in Cordoba of a new translation of Dioscorides *Materia Medica*. In addition Averroes (d. 1198) published a series of authoritative and widely read commentaries on the works of Aristotle.[5]

However despite the outstanding achievements of these gifted individuals in the Muslim world, no sustained scientific movement developed, partly because these writers' works did not find their way into the mainstream of Islamic education and, in particular, into the curriculum of the expanding *madrasas* in the eleventh century.[6] The major contribution of Islam to the later development of science and culture in the West was the preservation of many ancient Greek texts in Arabic translation—such as the works of Plato, Aristotle, Euclid, Appolonius, Archimedes, Ptolemy and Galen—most of which had been lost in Europe after the fall of the Roman empire. Then, in Cordoba and Seville in the twelfth century, these works were translated from Arabic into Latin—the *lingua franca* of medieval Europe—and became the core of the new learning in the emerging Christian universities described above.

Subsequent developments in the Islamic world diverged from those in Western societies as different ideas and ideological principles began to dominate in the two societies. Evidence shows that the effects of alternative Islamic beliefs eventually led to major differences in scientific, technological and economic development.[7]

For example, in the early Islamic centuries, according to Lewis, there existed:

> ...a rule called *ijtihad*, the exercise of independent judgement, whereby Muslim scholars, theologians, and jurists were able to resolve problems of theology and law for which scripture and tradition provided no explicit answer. A large part of the corpus of Muslim theology and jurisprudence came into being in this way. In due course the process came to an end when all the questions had been answered; in the traditional formulation, 'the gate of *ijtihad* was closed' and henceforth no further exercise of independent judgement was required or permitted. All the answers were already there, and all that was needed was to follow and obey. One is tempted to seek a parallel in the development of Muslim science, where the exercise of independent judgement in early days produced a rich flowering of scientific activity and discovery but where, too, the gate of *ijtihad* was subsequently closed and a long period followed during which Muslim science consisted almost entirely of compilation and repetition.[8]

Other writers argue that there were always some Muslims who wanted to retain or revive *ijtihad*—for example Ibn Khaldun in the fourteenth century and Shah Waliyullah in India in the eighteenth century. There have also been twentieth and twenty-first century advocates of a renewal of *ijtihad* and some argue that 'the gate' has never been fully closed and that procedures always existed for the *'ulema'* to invoke it. Nevertheless the *de facto* situation for many centuries was that *taqlid* (imitation or blind adherence to tradition) predominated over independent judgement.

Epistemological principles: the ideological mode

Approaches to knowledge and truth in ideological societies are based on an ideological mode which tends to be closed, dogmatic and monolithic. What is deemed true is derived from an ideology that is not open to question. Facts and data are selected or repressed according to whether or not they conform to the ideological framework. Claims of revealed truth and infallibility are often made. Criteria of logic and evidence are of secondary importance. The concept of academic freedom, as it has been understood for centuries in both the medieval universities in Europe and modern universities in the West, is virtually unknown and close ideological control is maintained both of institutions and of individuals. In consequence the ideological mode is intolerant of criticism. Those who oppose it are not reasoned with but attacked unceasingly with annihilating language and even threats to their lives. The aim and often the result is an intellectual conformity which destroys the inherent curiosity and open debate of the academic mode.

There are enough similarities between traditional Islam up to the end of the ninth century and modern Islamism to allow them to be considered together. Indeed ibn Hanbal, the ninth century founder of one major school of Islamic law (see below), was critical of the wider and more eclectic cultural developments stemming from the great translation movement under the Abbasids[9] just as modern Islamists reject many attempts at eclectic developments within modernist or liberal Islam.

Along with Marxism, traditional Islam and Islamism represent the two main contemporary types of ideological society. They exhibit a direct, close and continuous interaction between politics, religion and all social and educational activities. They are frequently buttressed by persistent moralistic appeals to religious and political ideals. In thoroughgoing ideological societies it has been virtually impossible to mount any public defence of the idea that academic enquiry should be separate from politics or that politics should be separate from religion or ideology.

In comparisons with Western societies, difficulties arise because key words or terms—such as truth, knowledge, authority, scholar, education—have very different and sometimes opposite or incompatible meanings in these very different contexts.

These differences are summarised in Table 1 (pp. 27-8) in which the comparisons are stated somewhat starkly in the form of Weberian ideal types.

The evidence underpinning this analysis for Marxist societies is given in *Fried Snowballs* and the references the book contains,[10] but the case of ideological Islam needs further discussion.

Traditional Islam, Islamism and the ideological mode: concepts of truth, scholarship and education

For Muslims, truth is the word of Allah as recited to his Prophet Mohammed and recorded in the Koran. It is supplemented by the *hadith*—the sayings and actions of the Prophet as recorded by his followers forming what is known as the *sunnah* or way of Mohammed. Knowledge is knowledge of this finite and final revelation of the truth.

Allah's revelation to Mohammed was spoken and for many years the Koran was transmitted by word of mouth as were the Prophet's sayings or *hadith*. The compilation in writing of the Koran started soon after the death of Mohammed in 632[11] and the authoritative text today is believed to have been defined around 650, although some non-Muslim scholars argue that it continued to evolve over the next two centuries. Over about the same period the *hadith* were gradually revised, edited and authenticated by tracing chains of oral attribution or *isnad* back to Mohammed or his contemporaries. Major collections of *hadith* date from about 850-900: by al-Bukhari (810-870), Muslim Ibn al-Hajjaj (d. 875), Ibn Maja (d. 887), Abu Dawud (d. 889), al-Tirmidhi (d. 892) and al-Nasa'i (d. 975).[12]

For traditional Muslims, the criteria of truth are conformity with the words of the Koran, the *hadith* and *sunnah* and their account of the key events of early Islamic history. Formal criteria of validity and evidence as used by 'Western' scholars are secondary and are rejected if they conflict with these criteria. The main subjects of study for Muslims are therefore the Koran, the *hadith* and *sunnah*, Islamic sources and Islamic history, and Arabic—the language of the Koran; other subjects are subsidiary.[13]

A scholar—*'alim*—is one who is respected for his knowledge of the Koran, the *hadith*, and *sunnah*, Arabic and other Islamic sources. Collective authority is vested in all the scholars—the *'ulema'* who are deemed experts concerning the final revelation of the truth and its interpretation.

The concept of academic freedom as understood in the West is virtually unknown because Islamic precepts require a direct, close and continuous interaction between religion, politics and all academic and educational activities, with the final authority vested in the *'ulema'*.[14]

The aim of Islamic education is to produce devout Muslims. It follows that the main, and sometimes the sole, purpose of education in traditional Islam is the study of the Koran, the *hadith* and *sunnah* and related topics in the history of Islam together with Arabic—the language of the Koran and the *hadith*. The major subjects taught in the West—mathematics, the natural and social sciences, engineering, arts, philosophy, history, economics and languages—are secondary.[15]

Further Islamic precepts

The traditional Muslim view is that the Koran was revealed to Mohammed over more than 20 years—from about 610 to 632. So some verses and *sura* (or chapters) date from his earlier years in Mecca—up to 622—and some from his ten years (622-632) in Medina. Moreover many verses in the Koran say different things on the same or similar topics. Hence there is a need for a principle to resolve such ambiguities. This is the principle of *naskh* or abrogation by which some verses override or abrogate others. In general the verse last revealed to Mohammed overrides or abrogates all earlier revealed verses which means that verses or *suras* revealed in Medina are likely to override or abrogate those revealed in Mecca.[16] For example, according to Gabriel:

> There are at least 114 verses in the Koran that speak of love, peace and forgiveness, especially in the Surah titled 'The Heifer' (Surah 2:62, 109 (Medina)). But when Surah 9:5 (Medina) was revealed later, it cancelled out those previous verses. This verse states:
>
>> 'Fight and slay the Pagans wherever you find them, and seize them, beleaguer them, and lie in wait for them in every stratagem (of war); but if they repent, and establish regular prayers and practise regular charity, then open the way for them: for Allah is Oft-forgiving, Most Merciful.'
>
> This is known as the verse of the sword, and it explains that Muslims must fight anyone who chooses not to convert to Islam, whether they are inside or outside of Arabia.[17]

The *shari'a* or Islamic holy law—there is no other kind of law in traditional Islam—is also based on the Koran, the *hadith* and *sunnah* and is interpreted by the *'ulema'*. Within Sunni Islam there are four major schools of law—the Hanafi, the Maliki, the Shafii and the Hanbali[18] whose founders died in 767, 795, 820 and 855 respectively. Shi'a Islam has its own traditions which differ relatively little from the four Sunni schools.

Mohammed was succeeded by a line of four 'rightly guided' caliphs Abu Bakr (632-634), Umar (634-644), Uthman (644-656) and Ali (656-661) who was Mohammed's son-in-law.

According to Lewis:

> Of the four Righteous Caliphs who followed the Prophet in the headship of the Islamic community, three were murdered. The second Caliph, Umar, was stabbed by a Christian slave with a private grievance; learning this, the Caliph on his deathbed thanked God that he had not been murdered by one of the faithful. Even this consolation was denied to his successors Uthman and Ali, who were both struck down by Muslim Arabs—the first by a group of angry mutineers, the second by a religious fanatic. In both murders, the perpetrators saw themselves as tyrannicides, freeing the community from an unrighteous ruler—and both found others to agree with them.
>
> The issues crystallised in the course of the Muslim civil war that followed Uthman's death. Mu'awiya, the governor of Syria and kinsman of the murdered Caliph, demanded the punishment of the

regicides. Ali, who had succeeded as Caliph, was unable or unwilling to comply, and his supporters, to justify his inaction, claimed that no crime had been committed, Uthman had been an oppressor; his death was an execution, not a murder. The same argument was used by the extremist sect of the Kharijites to justify the murder of Ali himself a few years later.[19]

The death of Ali in 661 cemented the emerging split between the Shi'ite Muslims (Shi'a Ali—literally the party of Ali) whose caliphs were descended from Ali and hence directly from the family of the Prophet and the majority Sunni Muslims whose caliphs from here on were dynastic— first the Umayyads (661-750) and then the Abbasids (750-1258).[20]

A conflict of epistemological principles

There is a clear conflict between the approaches to know-ledge and truth in the academic and ideological modes. This has two major contemporary consequences—concerning traditional Islam and the academies and traditional Islam and science.

As Lewis puts it:

> There was a time when scholars and other writers in communist eastern Europe relied on writers and publishers in the free West to speak the truth about their history, their culture, and their predicament. Today it is those who told the truth, not those who concealed or denied it, who are respected and welcomed in these countries...

> ...historians in free countries have a moral and professional obligation not to shirk the difficult issues and subjects that some people would place under some sort of taboo; not to submit to voluntary censorship, but to deal with these matters fairly, honestly, without apologetics, without polemic, and, of course, competently. Those who enjoy freedom have a moral obligation to use that freedom for those who do not possess it.[21]

Traditional Islam therefore poses a challenge for the practitioners of the academic mode: whether they should accept the Islamic view of the inviolability of the Koran and the *hadith* or whether they should subject them to the same kind of academic scrutiny and criticism that the Bible and other Judaeo-Christian sources have received over the last two centuries.[22]

Some Western academics and writers have adopted the latter approach—including Wansbrough, Crone, Cook and Warraq in the second half of the last century and Goldziher and others in the nineteenth and early twentieth centuries.[23]

For example, in the 1970s Wansbrough wrote that:

...as a document susceptible to analysis by the instruments and techniques of Biblical criticism, it [the Koran] is virtually unknown.[24]

By the 1990s this is still true as Rippin notes:

I have often encountered individuals who come to the study of Islam with a background in the historical study of the Hebrew Bible or early Christianity, and who express surprise at the lack of critical thought that appears in introductory textbooks on Islam... To students acquainted with approaches such as source criticism, oral formulae composition, literary analysis and structuralism, all quite commonly employed in the study of Judaism and Christianity, such naive historical study seems to suggest that Islam is being approached with less than academic candour.[25]

Rippin later develops the point thus:

The basic methodological point of Wansbrough's works is to ask the prime question not usually posed in the study of Islam: What is the evidence? Do we have witnesses to the Muslim accounts of the formation of their own community in any early disinterested sources? The Koran (in the form collected 'between two covers' as we know it today) is a good example: What evidence is there for the historical accuracy of the traditional accounts of the compilation of that book shortly after the death of Mohammed?

The earliest non-Islamic source testifying to the existence of the Koran appears to stem from the eighth century. Indeed, early Islamic sources, at least those which do not seem to have as their prime purpose the defence of the integrity of the canon, would seem to witness that the text of the Koran may not have been totally fixed until the early part of the ninth century. Manuscript evidence does not allow for substantially earlier dating either... What Wansbrough has done has been to bring to the study of Islam and the Koran the same healthy scepticism developed within modern biblical studies (and modern historical studies in general)...[26]

The lack, thus far, of any significant number of Islamic scholars to embrace fully the academic mode and to apply its principles to the foundations of Islam is of fundamental importance in understanding the divisions which continue to exist between many Muslims and the people of Western societies. It is also a fundamental difference which needs to be recognised in any interfaith dialogue.

The ideological mode, traditional Islam and science

It is no accident that all the great scientific and technological discoveries of recent times—quantum mechanics, new elementary particles, uranium fission, antibiotics and most of the new, highly effective drugs, transistors, electronic computers, the development of highly productive strains in agriculture, the discovery of other components of the 'Green Revolution' and the creation of new technologies in agriculture, industry and construction—all of them happened outside our country.

Andrei Sakharov, *My Country and the World*, 1975[27]

This quotation from Andrei Sakharov describes the fate of science in the Soviet Union under ideological Marxism, but it could equally well have been written about the lack of scientific discoveries under traditional Islam since the scientific revolution of the seventeenth century.[28]

The irony is that during the early period of Islamic history there was an eclectic acceptance of cultural influences from other cultures—perhaps best shown by the massive translation effort from Greek and other languages into Arabic under the Abbasids in eighth century Baghdad[29] and the later translations in twelfth century Cordoba from Arabic into Latin which provided the texts that formed the curriculum of the medieval universities of Europe. Muslim scholars, as we have seen, also made significant advances in knowledge in mathematics, astronomy, optics, medicine and the development of scientific instruments such as the astrolabe.

John Habgood, former Archbishop of York,[30] quotes Professor Akbar Ahmed of Cambridge University:

He [Akbar Ahmed] describes how after the great period of intellectual dominance when Islamic scholars had preserved Greek philosophy for medieval Europe, Islam virtually rejected its Greek heritage and with it the spirit of criticism. He then adds, 'This rejection may help to explain the deep-rooted cultural and intellectual opposition to Islam in the West *where the ancient Greek still matters'*.[31]

Key questions

This discussion raises a number of key questions for academics and politicians in the West. First, should the ideological mode be recognised in the universities of the West? And secondly, should funding and sponsorship be accepted from sources that, implicitly or even explicitly, impose conditions which are inconsistent with the principles of the academic mode?

Table 1: Academic and Ideological Modes—Summary Chart of Ideal Types

	Academic Mode	Ideological Mode Traditional Islam and Islamism	Ideological Mode Marxism
Truth	Reliable coherent knowledge based on evidence about the human and natural world and the universe.	The word of Allah as revealed to his Prophet Mohammed and recorded in the Koran together with the sayings and actions of the Prophet as recorded in the *hadith* and *sunnah*.	The writings of Marx and other major figures—Lenin, Stalin, Mao—are authoritative and their final interpreter is the Communist Party.
Criteria of Truth	Logical coherence and the use of all available relevant evidence; public defence and criticism of claims to knowledge. Knowledge is always provisional and tentative and subject to revision in the light of new arguments and evidence.	Conformity with the words of the Koran, the *hadith* and the key events of Islamic history. Formal criteria of validity and evidence are often ignored or rejected as irrelevant if they conflict with Islamic principles.	Results must be assimilated into a Marxist framework. Formal criteria of validity and evidence are frequently ignored or rejected as merely 'relative' to a rival ideology.
Knowledge	That which is developed and continues to be developed using the above criteria.	Knowledge of the finite and final revelation of the truth as defined above by a closed community of '*ulema*'.	Approaches to knowledge and truth are closed, dogmatic and monolithic and are ultimately interpreted by a centralised Communist party.
Main Subjects of Study	Mathematics, the Natural Sciences, the Social Sciences, Engineering, Languages, Literatures, History, Philosophy and the Arts.	The Koran, the *hadith*, Islamic sources and history, and Arabic—the language of the Koran; other subjects are subsidiary.	Study of Marxism-Leninism and the works of Marx, Lenin, Stalin and Mao come first. All other subjects are authorised and often largely determined by the Ideology.

Table cont'd/

	Academic Mode	Ideological Mode Traditional Islam and Islamism	Ideological Mode Marxism
Scholar	One who uses, respects and helps to institutionalise the above academic criteria and is recognised by his peers as expert in an academic subject.	One who has knowledge of the Koran, the *hadith*, Arabic and other Islamic sources.	The concept does not exist. The nearest equivalent is the expert in the writings of Marx and Lenin and their interpreters who is accredited by the Party.
Authority	Vested in the collective academic community made up of scholars as defined above.	Vested in the *'ulema'* who are expert in the final revelation of the truth and its interpretation as defined above.	Vested in the Communist Party who are the guardians and interpreters of the Ideology.
Academic Freedom	Academic freedom is valued for both individuals and institutions provided it respects the academic authority of those who acknowledge and help to institutionalise the crucial criteria for the validation of knowledge.	Traditional Islamic and Islamist ideology requires a direct, close and continuous interaction between religion/politics and all academic and educational activities. Consequently the concept of academic freedom is virtually unknown.	Marxist-Leninist ideology requires a close ideological control over academic institutions, individual academics and all academic and educational activities. It is not possible to defend publicly the idea that academic enquiry and politics should be separate.
Education	The preservation and extension of knowledge and its transmission to the next generation; the cultivation of powers of critical analysis and of moral and religious values; and the presentation of a wide range of ideas so that individuals can make up their own minds. The aim and the result is to produce autonomous individuals who can think for themselves.	Education centrally involves learning to recite and read the Koran, to read and interpret the *hadith* and sunnah and other Islamic sources, and to study Arabic. The 'ulema' assert their moral right to determine in detail the educational experiences of the people. The aim is to produce devout Muslims. The result is a complete denial of critical free individual enquiry.	Education is dominated by Marxist-Leninist ideology. Curricula and books are all controlled centrally and contain strong compulsory ideological components. The state and the Party assert their moral right and duty to determine in detail the educational experiences of the people. The aim is to produce good Communists. The result is a complete denial of critical free individual enquiry.

3

Political and Social Structures

A comparison of Western and ideological societies

The social and political structures of modern Western societies embody the values of tolerance, pluralism and individual freedoms which are fundamental in political and economic institutions, in the cultural and religious spheres and, most crucially, in the institutions concerned with freedom of expression, communication and access to information. Like their academies, Western societies are relatively decentralised. Their institutions and values combine to provide complex checks and balances on the exercise of centralised power.

Ideological societies, by contrast, tend to be monolithic, fiercely intolerant of dissent, and, *de facto*, lacking in individual freedoms. Control is attempted over all aspects of life—political, economic, cultural, educational, religious— and is frequently enforced centrally in the name of the dominant ideology—traditional Islam, Islamism or Marxism. Freedom of expression and of access to information are extensively prevented since conformity with the dominant ideology is the central value. No effective checks exist on the exercise of power by the ruling or governing group.

Table 2 (pp. 47-49) compares the main features of Western societies and ideological societies—both Islamic and Marxist. As in Table 1 (pp. 27-28), these comparisons are stated somewhat starkly and are best regarded as Weberian ideal types.

Although much has been published about Western and Marxist societies,[1] few comparisons have been made between Western and Islamic societies.

Islamist criticisms of Western societies

The values of Western societies allow the public expression of criticism—including the destructive criticisms of ideologists who would undermine and destroy the foundations of the societies themselves.

Islamists take advantage of the freedoms of Western societies to publicise their criticisms, including allegations that Western societies are morally decadent; are inherently and fundamentally prejudiced against Islam and Muslims; launched the medieval Crusades in a bid to eliminate Islam and are now launching a modern crusade with the same aim; support the state of Israel; and are allies of America which has based troops in the Islamic holy land of Saudi Arabia since 1990. The extent to which these allegations may or may not be justified is open to question.

But there is an asymmetry of criticism which is not justifiable in terms of the Western academic mode. Islamist Muslims show a great reluctance to apply their wide ranging criticisms of Western societies to Islamic societies—either those which have existed over the centuries or modern Islamic states. This refusal to compare cannot be justified given the evidence available from the historical experience of fourteen centuries of Islamic societies and the many modern Islamic states.

It is therefore one of the main purposes of this paper to indicate the existence of a body of evidence about Islamic societies against which the Muslims' major criticisms of Western societies can be judged. Such evidence, like all evidence, will be incomplete. But in its totality it constitutes a challenge which critics of Western societies, including both Islamist and non-Islamist Muslims, should be encouraged to answer.

Political, legal and social institutions in traditional Islamic and Islamist societies

Traditional Islamic societies differ radically from Western societies in that virtually all aspects of such societies—including religious, political, economic, social, judicial and military matters—are very closely interlinked. There has been virtually no acceptance of the separate development of civil society. Nor, crucially, has there been any significant recognition that society and its institutions may continually change, develop, evolve or improve in response to changing circumstances.[2]

This is in clear contrast to the way in which both the secular and religious aspects of society in the Judaeo-Christian tradition have changed and evolved over time. For example, Islam does not make the distinction between the secular and the sacred exemplified in the Biblical text:

> Render unto God the things that are God's and to Caesar the things that are Caesar's.[3]

The comprehensive control by religion of virtually every aspect of human life, individual and collective, enshrines the essence of totalitarianism and totalitarian control which is inherently incompatible with the concept of individual freedom which lies at the heart of liberal democracy.

In addition, traditional Islamic and Islamist societies are profoundly influenced by two all-embracing concepts —*shari'a* and *jihad*.

Shari'a

This is the name given to the system of Islamic law which was developed in early Islamic societies and which in one form or another is often urged on societies in the modern world if they are to be truly Islamic. It is sometimes translated as 'holy law' but for traditional Muslims:

> ...the adjective is tautologous. The *shari'a* is simply the law, and there is no other. It is holy in that it derives from God, and is the external and unchangeable expression of God's commandments to mankind.[4]

The main features of the *shari'a* are indicated in this description by Kramer of the aims of modern Islamists:

> ...a virtuous government, they affirm, can rest only on obedience to the divinely-given law of Islam, the *shari'a*... which is not legislated but revealed law; as such, in the eyes of the fundamentalists it has already achieved perfection, and while it is not above some reinterpretation, neither is it infinitely elastic.

> (The *shari'a* contains) principled affirmations of inequality, primarily between Muslims and non-Muslims, secondarily between men

and women. This has made fundamentalists into the most unyielding critics of the Universal Declaration of Human Rights, which guarantees the freedom to choose one's religion and one's spouse. Both freedoms indisputably contradict Islamic law, which defines conversion out of Islam as a capital offence, and forbids marriage between a Muslim woman and a non-Muslim man...

The *shari'a*, as a perfect law, cannot be abrogated or altered, and certainly not by the shifting moods of an electorate. Accordingly, every major fundamentalist thinker has repudiated popular sovereignty as a rebellion against God, the sole legislator. In the changed circumstances of the 1990s, some activists do allow that an election can serve a useful one-time purpose, as a collective referendum of allegiance to Islam, and as an act of submission to a regime of divine justice. But once such a regime gains power, its true measure is not how effectively it implements the will of the people but how efficiently it applies Islamic law.[5]

Jihad

Jihad is a word which has various meanings. Literally it means 'struggle', including 'struggle for the good Islamic life', but is frequently translated as Holy War and it often means 'violent' Holy War. Islamist literature frequently mentions *jihad* for various purposes but the ambiguity of the term makes it capable of different interpretations.

According to Lewis, *jihad* is:

...an Arabic word with the literal meaning of 'effort', 'striving', or 'struggle'. In the Qur'an and still more the Traditions commonly though not invariably followed by the words 'in the path of God', it has usually been understood as meaning 'to wage war'. The great collections of *hadith* all contain a section devoted to *jihad* in which the military meaning predominates. The same is true of the classical manuals of *shari'a* law. There were some who argued that *jihad* should be understood in a moral and spiritual, rather than a military, sense. Such arguments were sometimes put forward by Shi'ite theologians in classical times, and more frequently by modernisers and reformists in the nineteenth and twentieth centuries. The overwhelming majority of classical theologians, jurists, and traditionalists, however, understood the obligation of *jihad* in a military sense, and have examined and expounded it accordingly.

Moreover:

...*jihad*, is one of the basic commandments of the faith, an obligation imposed on all Muslims by God, through revelation... The basis of the obligation of *jihad* is the universality of the Muslim revelation. God's word and God's message are for all mankind; it is the duty of those who have accepted them to strive (*jahada*) unceasingly to convert or at least to subjugate those who have not. This obligation is without limit of time or space. It must continue until the whole world has either accepted the Islamic faith or submitted to the power of the Islamic state.

Until that happens, the world is divided into two: the House of Islam (*dar al-Islam*), where Muslims rule and the law of Islam prevails; and the House of War (*dar al-Harb*), comprising the rest of the world. Between the two there is a morally necessary, legally and religiously obligatory state of war, until the final and inevitable triumph of Islam over unbelief. According to the law books, this state of war could be interrupted, when expedient, by an armistice or truce of limited duration. It could not be terminated by a peace, but only by a final victory.[6]

Jihad is also waged against apostates. An apostate—or *murtadd*:

...is one who had been or had become a Muslim, and then had abandoned Islam and adopted another faith or, more commonly, reverted to his previous or ancestral faith. By so doing, he has renounced his allegiance to the Muslim state, and thus has become an enemy against whom it is legitimate, even obligatory, to wage war...

...the Muslim who abandons his faith is ... not only a renegade; he is a traitor, and the law insists that he must be punished as such. The jurists agreed on the need to execute the apostate individual, and to make war against the apostate state.

The rules of warfare against the apostate are very much harsher than those governing warfare against the unbeliever. He may not be given quarter or safe conduct, and no truce or agreement with him is permissible...

The only options before him are recantation or death. He may choose to return to Islam, in which case his offence committed during his apostasy will be pardoned and his confiscated property—or what remains of it—be returned to him. If he refuses, he must be put to death by the sword.[7]

Jihad and the Koran

A key development in the concept of *jihad* is contained in this verse in the Koran:

Fight those who believe not in Allah, nor the Last Day, nor hold that forbidden which has been forbidden by Allah and His Prophet, nor

acknowledge the religion of truth [i.e. Islam] among the People of the
Book (Jews and Christians), until they pay the *jizya* [tax] with
willing submission, and feel themselves subdued.

Surah 9:29, (Medina)

In other words Muslims must fight unbelievers, those who
allow things Allah forbids, and Jews and Christians unless
they pay the *jizya* tax. The options for other unbelievers are
to accept Islam or be killed.

Paradise and jihad

Muslims believe that when they die they go to the grave to
await the day of judgement when Allah will decide, on the
basis of works done on earth, who goes to Paradise and who
to hell.[8] The only way to guarantee going to Paradise—and
avoid Allah's verdict on the day of judgement—is to die in
jihad while fighting the enemies of Islam.[9] This provides a
major religious motive for suicide bombers or others to
volunteer for *jihad*.[10] Moreover many verses in the Koran—and especially those revealed in Medina—deal with
jihad which, according to Gabriel: 'became the basic power
and driving force of Islam'.[11]

In Mohammed's time, *jihad* was practised regularly
against Christians and Jews as well as against those who
did not convert to Islam.[12] As the Koran says:

...if they turn renegades, seize them and slay them wherever ye find
them...   Surah 4:89, (Medina)[13]

The ultimate aim of *jihad* is to establish Islamic authority
over the whole world as indicated by this Koranic verse
received by Mohammed in Medina:

And fight with them on until there is no more tumult and oppression, And there prevail justice and faith in Allah all together and
everywhere...   Surah 8:39, (Medina)

Over 22 years (610-632), Mohammed's precepts in the
Koran changed from fight those who persecute you to fight
those who reject Islam in Arabia and then to the final
command of *jihad*—conquer the world in the name of Islam.
No subsequent Koranic verse contradicted this final command of *jihad* so it must be deemed to remain as a goal of
Islam today.

Mohammed himself led 27 battles and authorised nearly twice as many more during his ten years in Medina (622-632)—a rate of about seven battles a year—and after his death the Muslims rapidly put these precepts into practice successfully taking *jihad* to many countries outside Arabia.

Jihad and the background to the Crusades

Over the succeeding years and centuries military *jihad* was remarkably successful. Starting with the capture of Jerusalem from the Christians in 638 and followed by the capture of much of Spain by 715—a conquest which did not finally end until the fall of Granada in 1492, nearly 800 years later—Islam first conquered and then converted much of Europe, North Africa and Asia. Overall this *jihad* lasted nearly 1,300 years, until the nineteenth century, interrupted only by about 200 years of resistance during the Crusades (1096-1270).[14]

As Lewis puts it:

For roughly a thousand years, from the first irruption of the Muslim armies into the Christian lands of the Levant in the early seventh century until the second and final Turkish withdrawal from the walls of Vienna in 1683, European Christendom lived under the constant and imminent menace of Islam. The very first Islamic expansion took place largely at Christian expense: Syria, Palestine, Egypt, and North Africa were all Christian countries, provinces of the Christian Roman Empire or subject to other Christian rulers, until they were incorporated in the realm of the caliphs. Their lands were lost to the conquering armies of Islam, their peoples to the militant faith of the conquerors. The Muslim advance continued into Europe not once, but three times. The first wave of Muslim expansion into Europe began in the early years of the eighth century and for a while engulfed Spain, Portugal, southern Italy, and even parts of France. It did not end until 1492, with the defeat and extinction of the last Muslim state on west European soil. The second wave struck eastern Europe when the Mongols of the Golden Horde, who had established their domination over Russia and most of eastern Europe, were converted to Islam and subjected Muscovy and the other Russian principalities to the suzerainty of a Muslim overlord. That, too, was ended after a long and bitter struggle by a Christian reconquest and the withdrawal of the Islamized Tartars from Russia. The third wave was that of the Seljuk and Ottoman Turks, who, after conquering Anatolia from the Byzantine Empire, crossed into Europe and established a mighty empire in the Balkan

Peninsula. In the course of their advance, the Turks captured Constantinople and twice laid siege to Vienna, while the vessels of the Barbary corsairs carried the naval *jihad* as far as the British Isles and, on one occasion, even Iceland. It was the second siege of Vienna and the defeat and retreat of the Ottoman forces that marked the real turning point in the relations between the two religions and civilisations.[15]

The Crusades therefore were a response to four hundred years of aggression and expansion of Islam by war. While actions were carried out by both sides which are unacceptable by the standards of modern Western societies,[16] it is important to understand them in context. They were a long-delayed military response to centuries of conquest by *jihad* in which many Christians were martyred and lands which had been Christian for centuries—such as Byzantium and much of the Mediterranean—were conquered and ruled by Islam.

Human rights and freedoms in traditional Islamic and Islamist societies

Mayer has compared the 1948 Universal Declaration of Human Rights of the United Nations with a number of documents setting out Islam's attitude to alternative ideologies and dissent:

- a pamphlet by Mawdudi (a Pakistani Islamist who died in 1979—see below);

- the 1981 Universal Islamic Declaration of Human Rights;

- a draft Islamic Constitution published by Al-Azhar University in Cairo;

- and the 1979 Iranian Constitution.[17]

In summary, Mayer concludes that:

The authors of these Islamic human rights schemes do not see the relationship of the individual and the state as being an adversarial one in which the weaker party, the individual, needs iron-clad guarantees of civil and political rights to offset the tendencies of modern governments to assert their powers at the expense of the freedoms of the individual. Furthermore, they seem to believe that where the freedom of the individual and the religious values of the traditional culture are in conflict, it is the former that should give way.

...the *shari'a* criteria that are employed to restrict rights are left so uncertain and general that they... afford no means for protecting the individual against deprivations of the rights that are guaranteed by international law. Thereby the stage is set not just for the diminution of these rights but potentially for denying them altogether.[18]

This position contrasts with the way that many Islamist and non-Islamist Muslims use or exploit the laws—based on human rights—of Western societies.

Freedom of religion and apostasy

The traditional Islamic response to Muslims who seek to change their religion is recantation or death (see p. 33 above). There is no indication that any of the modern Islamic authorities analysed by Mayer regard this as a problem:

...The failure of a single one of these Islamic human rights schemes to take a position against the application of the *shari'a* death penalty for apostasy means that the authors of these schemes have neglected to confront and resolve the main issues involved in harmonising international human rights and *shari'a* standards.

...The authors' unwillingness to repudiate the rule that a person should be executed over a question of religious belief reveals the enormous gap that exists between their mentalities and the modern philosophy of human rights.[19]

The status of women

The status of women within Islam is a matter of diverse interpretations. What is clear is that women are subject to considerable limitations on what they can do compared with men, both in private in the home and in public. In courts of law on many key issues the testimony of one man is equivalent to that of two women.[20]

Gabriel sums up the teachings of the Koran relating to women:

1. A Muslim man can be married to four women at the same time, but a Muslim woman can only be married to one man. 'Marry (other) women of your choice, two or three, or four' (Surah 4:3, [Medina]).

2. Men have the right to ask for a divorce, but not women (Surah 2:229 [Medina]).

3. Women only inherit half of what men inherit (Surah 4:11 [Medina]).

4. Women may not serve as imams, and they are not allowed to lead prayer in the presence of men. (Man must always be above woman according to Surah 4:34 [Medina]).

5. A woman is not allowed to answer the door at home if her husband is not there, even if it's her brother or a relative at the door. (This is derived from Surah 33:53 [Medina], where Mohammed was giving instructions to people who visited his home. He said that if he wasn't home, they had to speak to his wives through a screen.)

6. Women should stay in their houses (Surah 33:33 [Medina]). Many Muslim women cannot travel without the permission of their fathers or husbands.

7. If a wife refuses to have sexual relations with her husband, it is permissible for the husband to physically beat her until she submits (Surah 4:34 [Medina]).[21]

Most Islamic authorities do not seem to regard the inequality in women's rights as a problem. According to Mayer:

> ...there is an absence of any willingness to recognise women as full, equal human beings who deserve the same rights and freedoms as men. Instead, discrimination against women is treated as something entirely natural...[22]

The rights of non-Muslims and Dhimmi status

Throughout the history of Islamic societies non-Muslims have been given a less advantageous status than Muslims. This system has applied most frequently to Jews and Christians. They were able to live within Islamic societies, mostly in peace, provided they accepted *dhimmi* status which was a kind of second class status. *Dhimmi* status involved paying a special tax and having considerably limited legal rights compared with Muslims—for example in the ability to own property or to carry out certain occupations. In Islamic courts of law they are not allowed to give evidence against Muslims and sometimes have to pay a Muslim to give evidence for them.[23]

In Mayer's analysis of these Islamic documents she argues that:

> ...to the extent that they deal with the question of the rights of religious minorities, they seem to endorse premodern *shari'a* rules that call for non-Muslims to be relegated to an inferior status if they qualify as members of the *ahl al-kitab* (i.e. Jews or Christians) and for them to be treated as nonpersons if they do not qualify for such inclusion. The Azhar draft constitution avoids dealing with the status of non-Muslims. In the context of a document that seems to support the general applicability of premodern *shari'a* rules, the failure to address the issue suggests that the intent was to retain such rules to govern the status of non-Muslims.[24]

Slavery

Slavery has been associated with some Islamic societies for at least a thousand years and continues to be so into the twenty-first century.[25] The case of Sudan is particularly well documented.[26]

Pipes describes in detail the use of slaves as soldiers within Islam:

> For a full millennium, from the early 3rd/9th century until the early 13th/19th, Muslims regularly and deliberately employed slaves as soldiers. This occurred through nearly the whole of Islamdom, from Central Africa to Central Asia, from Spain to Bengal, and perhaps beyond.... Even a cursory glance at the history of Muslim peoples reveals the extraordinary role played by men of slave origins in the armed forces. They served both as soldiers and as officers, then often acquired pre-eminent roles in administration, politics, and all aspects of public affairs. The systematic use of slaves as soldiers constituted the single most distinctive feature of Islamicate public life in premodern times...[27]

Moreover there is ample evidence of the existence of slavery and slave trades within Islam, with major growth taking place in the eighteenth and nineteenth centuries:

> The trans-Saharan slave trade increased in volume during the eighteenth and nineteenth centuries. Ottoman rulers in league with Muslim Bornu transported large numbers of slaves across the Sahara into the then Ottoman Empire. Many eyewitness accounts talk of substantial loss of lives during the raids and journeys into servitude.[28]

There is some evidence that the scale of the intra-African slave trade is substantially greater in total than that of the Atlantic slave trade which peaked in the eighteenth century and was gradually abolished from the early nineteenth century onwards.

> Apart from the high loss of lives during the raids and journeys, conservative estimates suggest that between 11 and 14 million Africans were transported into Muslim lands.[29]

Yet the number of studies which have been made of the intra-African slave trade is minute in comparison to the voluminous discussion of the Atlantic slave trade.[30]

Where slavery has been abolished or diminished in Islamic societies this has almost always been at the instigation of or under pressure from colonial European powers:

> The anti-slavery measures of European colonial powers were generally viewed by Muslims not only as a threat to their very livelihood but also an affront to their religion... Muslims therefore resisted all abolition efforts and chattel slavery persists in Muslim countries today.[31]

A fascinating debate in the House of Lords in 1960 provided first hand evidence on slavery and the slave trade in Africa and Arabia in the mid-twentieth century.[32]

More recently:

> In a report presented by the Secretary General to the United Nations General Assembly in October 1995, the abduction and traffic of young boys and girls from Southern Sudan to the northern part of the country for sale as servants and concubines is highlighted in several paragraphs.[33]

Recent studies show that within the northern Nigerian context:

> ...people can still be found who are considered slaves ... The death of slavery, pronounced by so many observers, has been a protracted one and is still not over.[34]

Moreover, according to Gordon:

> To many Arabs, the issue of slavery is a source of discomfort. To speak out against it would be to impugn a tenet of Koranic law; to condone slavery would give offence to Africans whose ancestors and not-too-distant relatives in recent times fell victim to Arab slave traders and their agents. As a result, they instinctively keep silent on the subject, which to this day is a source of pain and humiliation for many Africans.[35]

Finally in discussing slavery it is worth remembering that:

> ...it was Europe ... that first decided to set the slaves free: at home, then in the colonies, and finally in all the world. Western technology made slavery unnecessary; Western ideas made it intolerable. There have been many slaveries, but there has been only one abolition, which eventually shattered even the rooted and ramified slave systems of the Old World.[36]

Media of communication in traditional Islamic and Islamist societies

In most Islamic societies, freedom of expression and of access to information are frequently prevented since conformity with the dominant ideology is the central value.

It is very difficult for alternative views to be heard and much of the media in many Islamic countries operates under close government scrutiny and even censorship.

One problem in assessing the content and tone of the media in these countries is that few in the West can read, for example, Arabic or Farsi. Therefore the work of the Middle East Media Research Institute (MEMRI) is invaluable in providing translations of current news coverage in, for example, *al-Ahram*—the leading Egyptian government daily newspaper—and other comparable publications.[37]

Two revealing articles are:

- 'Accursed Forever and Ever' from the Egyptian government daily *Al-Ahram*—a virulently anti-Jewish article which MEMRI headlined as 'Columnist for Egyptian Government Daily to Hitler: "If Only You Had Done It, Brother"' (3 May 2002);

- an article headlined '72 Black Eyed Virgins: A Muslim Debate on the Rewards of Martyrs' debating the nature of Paradise for Muslims as described in the Koran and the *hadith* (30 October 2001).

Economies in traditional Islamic and Islamist societies

Islamic societies have experienced limited economic freedom and relatively less economic success compared with many non-Muslim countries. In particular the lack of provision under Islamic law for independent corporations—see the discussion of medieval universities in Chapter 2—and the prohibition on interest and its description as usury[38] have severely limited economic development throughout Islam both historically and in modern times.

Currently this lack of success is indicated by the lists of countries ranked by the World Bank according to their economic prosperity as shown by estimates of Gross National Income per head.[39] The list of just over 200 countries includes 38 Muslim countries—seven of which appear in the top 100 and 31 in the bottom hundred. The only two Muslim countries in the top 50 are Brunei (22nd) and United Arab Emirates (32nd) with Saudi Arabia third in 62nd place; the relative economic prosperity of these three countries is primarily due to oil revenues from Western oil companies rather from indigenous economic development.

Further evidence is provided by the Arab Human Development Report 2002 published by the United Nations Development Programme (UNDP) and largely written by economists from Arab countries. The report deplores the relative economic backwardness of the Arab world and outlines some possible reasons for this. For example:

Aspirations for Freedom and Democracy Remain Unfulfilled

There is a substantial lag between Arab countries and other regions in terms of participatory governance. The wave of democracy that transformed governance in most of Latin America and East Asia in 1980s and Eastern Europe and much of Central Asia in the late 1980s and early 1990s has barely reached the Arab States. This freedom deficit undermines human development and is one of the most painful manifestations of lagging political development. While *de jure* acceptance of democracy and human rights is enshrined in constitutions, legal codes and government pronouncements, *de facto* implementation is often neglected and, in some cases, deliberately disregarded.

In most cases, the governance pattern is characterized by a powerful executive branch that exerts significant control over all other branches of the state, being in some cases free from institutional checks and balances. Representative democracy is not always genuine and sometimes absent. Freedoms of expression and association are frequently curtailed. Obsolete norms of legitimacy prevail.[40]

In addition:

Women's literacy rates have expanded threefold since 1970; female primary and secondary enrolment rates have more than doubled. However, these achievements have not succeeded in countering gender-based social attitudes and norms that exclusively stress women's reproductive role and reinforce the gender-based asymmetry of unpaid care. As a consequence, more than half of Arab women are still illiterate. The region's maternal mortality rate is double that of Latin America and the Caribbean, and four times that of East Asia.

Women also suffer from unequal citizenship and legal entitlements, often evident in voting rights and legal codes. The utilization of Arab women's capabilities through political and economic participation remains the lowest in the world in quantitative terms, as evidenced by the very low share of women in parliaments, cabinets, and the work force and in the trend towards the feminization of unemployment. Qualitatively, women suffer from inequality of opportunity, evident in employment status, wages and gender-based occupational segregation. Society as a whole suffers when a huge proportion of its productive potential is stifled, resulting in lower family incomes and standards of living.

Bridled minds, shackled potential

About 65 million adult Arabs are illiterate, two thirds of them women. Illiteracy rates are much higher than in much poorer countries. This challenge is unlikely to disappear quickly. Ten million children between 6 and 15 years of age are currently out of school; if current trends persist, this number will increase by 40 per cent by 2015. The challenge is far more than overcoming the under-supply of knowledge to people. Equally important is overcoming the under-supply of knowledgeable people, a problem exacerbated by the low quality of education together with the lack of mechanisms for intellectual capital development and use.[41]

Finally:

Traditional culture and values, including traditional Arab culture and values, can be at odds with those of the globalizing world.[42]

and:

Moving towards pluralism, which is more conducive to genuine sustainable participation and in tune with the requirements of today's and tomorrow's world, needs to become a priority for Arab countries.[43]

No mention is made throughout the report of Islam being involved in any way at all as a factor in influencing economic development. However, the report does mention war and occupation in the Middle East as major factors in its economic underdevelopment. In addition, Islamic economies have been and remain strongly dependent on the import of science and technology from the West—a subject which was briefly discussed in Chapter 2 and to which we now return.

Education, science and technology in traditional Islamic and Islamist societies

Education was briefly discussed in Chapter 2 but will now be considered in more detail as it is of central importance to the main themes of this book.

After the initial flourishing of the study of science in Abbasid Baghdad following the translation of many ancient Greek texts, there were considerable impediments to its continuing growth within Islam.

According to Huff:

> ...the sciences we call the natural sciences were called the foreign sciences by the Muslims. In contrast the so-called Islamic sciences were those devoted to the study of the Koran, the traditions of the Prophet (*hadith*), legal knowledge (*fiqh*), theology (*kalam*), poetry, and the Arabic language...[44]

This meant:

> ...the exclusion of the sciences of the ancients from the curriculum of the schools of higher learning.[45] The bedrock of instruction was Islamic law (*fiqh*), along with Koranic studies, Arabic, grammar, the sciences of tradition (*hadith*), and enough arithmetic to equip legists and qadis to divide up inheritances.[46]

Huff also argues that the *madrasas*—at the time the main Islamic institutions of higher learning[47]—were Islamic charitable trusts which under Islamic law could only devote resources to Islamic purposes:

> ...they were religious endowments that legally had to follow the wishes, religious or otherwise, of their founders. However, the law of trust (the law of *waqf*) specifically forbade appropriating property and funds through the institutions of *waqf* for purposes other than those sanctified by Islam. This stipulation is... a major legal

impediment to the unfolding of intellectual and organisational evolution in the Islamic world...[48]

According to Sabra:

...in Islam, whether in ninth- and tenth-century Baghdad, eleventh-century Egypt and central Asia, twelfth-century Spain, thirteenth-century Maragha in north-western Iran, or fifteenth-century Samarkand, the major scientific work associated with the names of those who were active at those times and places was carried out under the patronage of rulers whose primary interests lay in the practical benefits promised by the practitioners of medicine and astronomy and astrology and applied mathematics.[49]

Many technical innovations which spread rapidly in Europe were restricted or even banned in Islamic countries. One example is the printing press, which was banned in Islamic lands for many centuries after its appearance in the West.[50]

Islamic countries also showed considerable reluctance to adopt new technologies, even those involved in waging war. According to Lewis:

Though gunpowder had been invented centuries earlier in China, the dubious credit for recognising and realising its military potential belongs to Christian Europe. The Muslim lands were at first reluctant to accept this new device. It would appear that guns were used in the defence of Aleppo when it was besieged by Timberline, but in general the Mamluks of Egypt and Syria rejected a weapon which they found unchivalrous and which they realised to be destructive of their social order. The Ottomans were much quicker to appreciate the value of firearms, and it was largely thanks to their use of musketry and cannon that they were able to defeat their two major Muslim rivals, the sultan of Egypt and the shah of Persia. The effective use of cannon played an important part in the conquest of Constantinople in 1453 and in other victories won by the Ottomans over both their European and their Muslim adversaries. Significantly, the majority of their gun-founders and gunners were European renegades or adventurers. While the Ottomans were well able to deploy this new weapon, they continued to rely on outsiders for the science and even the technology needed to produce it... The inevitable result was that, with the passage of time, the Ottoman artillery fell steadily behind that of their European rivals.

Later:

...when a Venetian war galley ran aground in Turkish waters, Ottoman naval engineers examined it with great interest and wished to incorporate several features of its construction and armament in their own ships. The question was put to the chief Mufti of the capital—is it licit to copy the devices of the infidels in such matters? The reply came that in order to defeat the infidel it is permissible to imitate the weapons of the infidel.

The question raised is an important one. In the Muslim tradition, innovation is generally assumed to be bad unless it can be shown to be good. The word *bid'a*, innovation or novelty, denotes a departure from the sacred precept and practice communicated to mankind by the Prophet, his disciples, and the early Muslims. Tradition is good and enshrines God's message to mankind. Departure from tradition is therefore bad, and in time the word *bid'a*, among Muslims, came to have approximately the same connotation as heresy in Christendom.[51]

Concerning more modern times Huff reports that:

...as recently as the mid-1980s, concerned Muslim intellectuals lamented the fact that modern science had not taken root in the Islamic countries of the world, with the consequence that there is no Islamic Hong Kong, Singapore, or Japan.[52] According to the Abdus Salam, president of the Third World Academy of Science, 'of all civilisations of this planet, science is weakest in the lands of Islam'.[53] The reason given for this is that 'secular', 'Western', and 'Eastern' science and technology have no basis in [the] Islamic ethos and Muslim culture. Their adoption makes Muslims less Islamic.[54] More simply put, modern science is perceived as un-Islamic, and those who embrace it are thought to have taken a first and fatal step toward impiety. It was for this reason that like-minded Muslims founded the Muslim Association for the Advancement of Science in 1985. According to these Muslims, all scientific ideas must be shown to be consistent with, if not derived from, the *shari'a*.[55]

These are some of the reasons why the Pakistani Nobel prize-winning physicist, Abdus Salam, chose to live and work abroad rather than in his own country.[56]

The record of the award of Nobel prizes for physics, chemistry and medicine shows that the approximately 1.2 billion Muslims who comprise around 20 per cent of the world's population have received no more than half a dozen such prizes. By contrast, the approximately 14 million Jews, who comprise around 0.2 per cent of the world's population, have received nearly one hundred—nearly 20 times as many absolutely and more than a thousand times as many relatively.

Table 2: Western Societies and Ideological Societies—Summary Chart of Ideal

	Western Societies	Ideological Traditional Islamic and Islamist Societies	Ideological Marxist Societies
Social and Political	Western societies are decentralised. The political, educational, cultural, religious and economic spheres of human life are partially separated and pluralism is encouraged and realised. There are a number of political parties and free elections by secret ballot.	Ideologically Islamic/Islamist societies are monolithic, intolerant of dissent, and, *de facto*, lacking in individual freedoms. Control is attempted over all aspects of life in the name of Islam. Constitutions, where they exist, frequently have apparently liberal clauses overridden by clauses requiring conformity with *shari'a* law. Religion and politics are completely intertwined so that a range of competing political parties on the Western model is very unlikely.	Marxist societies are centralised, monolithic and attempt to control all aspects of life via the official Marxist ideology. Alternative political programmes are defined *de facto* as treason or mental disorder. Elections have only a single list of Communist Party candidates. Constitutions have apparently liberal clauses overridden by clauses condemning opposition to Party or ideology.
Legal	There is a diffusion of power with the partial separation of legislative, executive and judicial processes. Both statute law and common law can be modified and evolve over time as can holy or canon law.	No effective checks exist on the exercise of power by the 'ulema' or the ruling group. The legal system is dominated by the *shari'a* or Islamic Holy Law, derived from the Koran and the *hadith*; there is no other kind of law.	Judicial and legal systems are totally subservient to the Communist Party and are used to enforce ideological conformity by both physical and psychological sanctions. The result has been millions of deaths and the indefinite confinement of millions more in forced labour camps.

table cont'd/

	Western Societies	Ideological Traditional Islamic and Islamist Societies	Ideological Marxist Societies
Use of Force	Governments have a monopoly in the use of force for defence against external enemies and to maintain order. This monopoly is subject to and controlled by the powers exercised by the legislature and independent judiciary.	*Jihad* or Holy War is an obligation—imposed by Allah on all Muslims—to strive unceasingly to convert or to subjugate non-Muslims. *Jihad* is without limit of time or space and continues until the whole world accepts Islam or submits to the Islamic state. The use of force internally is subject to the *sharia* .	Governments have a monopoly in the use of force to maintain order and for defence against external enemies. No effective restraints on the use of force are exercised by the legislature or the judiciary which are completely subservient to the government or Party .
Alternative Ideologies and Dissent	The values of pluralism, openness and tolerance pervade the cultural, religious and moral spheres; there is freedom of worship with many coexisting religions—together with a similar freedom for non-believers.	*Dhimmi* or second-class status has traditionally been available to Jews and Christians in Islamic societies. *Dhimmis* pay a special tax and have very limited legal rights. Apostates have a stark choice—to re-convert to Islam or to die.	Religions and national or ethnic groups are severely repressed if they challenge the hegemony of the Party. Experimental movements in art or literature are regarded as counter-revolutionary and are suppressed.
Inequalities	There are commitments to equality before the law and to political equality for all citizens. Nevertheless, inequalities of status, opportunity and reward persist.	*Sharia* law requires inequalities between Muslims and: (i) Christians/Jews; (ii) all other non-Muslims; and between men and women. Slavery has been endemic in the Muslim world for centuries and still continues. Substantial inequalities of opportunity and reward persist.	Party members enjoy enormous economic, social and educational privileges. Very large inequalities persist in spite of an ideological commitment to equality and much greater restrictions on liberty than exist in Western societies.

table cont'd/

	Western Societies	Ideological Traditional Islamic and Islamist Societies	Ideological Marxist Societies
Media of Communication	There is freedom of public debate, open criticism and pluralism in the press, television, radio, the cinema, the arts and publishing, subject to legal limitations on libel and on incitement to violence or racial hatred.	Freedom of expression and of access to information are frequently severely limited or prevented since conformity with the dominant Ideology is the central value.	All information sources—including literature, art and educational textbooks—are directly controlled by the Propaganda departments of the Communist Party. The media exist not to provide information but to propagate Party ideology.
Economies	There is a diffusion of economic power between state and private ownership. Economic freedoms are exercised within a free or open market whose functioning closely involves freedom of information and the freedoms to travel, to change jobs and to choose where to live.	Traditional Islamic and Islamist principles require limited economic freedom which results in limited economic success compared with many non-Muslim countries. Islamic economies are strongly dependent on the import of science and technology from the West and, in many cases, on an imported oil industry.	State ownership of all the means of production and central planning of the economy result in economic inefficiencies and shortages which reinforce the need to restrict information so as to prevent discontent. Communist economies have been strongly dependent on the import of science and technology from the West.

4

Conflicts between Western and Islamic Societies: past and present

Modern Western societies, and the academies they nurture, are freer, more open and more successful intellectually, economically and politically than are closed societies in which all institutions are dominated by an ideological mode. These perceived disparities frequently lead ideological societies to try to undermine or even destroy the Western societies they have so far failed to emulate scientifically or economically.

Their peoples, who suffer relative deprivation compared with Western societies, may feel humiliated and resentful and become vulnerable to recruitment to fanatical causes. This humiliation, in case of Islam, is often reinforced by the memories of earlier periods in history when Islamic countries successfully, and often continuously, expanded their domains and were a major force in the world.

All these factors contribute to contemporary attacks on Western societies in terms of the ideology underpinning such attacks; the strategy involved; and the ways, means and tactics employed.[1]

Ideology

Current antagonism to the West in Islamic countries has a long history, starting with the early encounters with modernity and the West in the colonial era right up to modern times. It has led to frequent attempts to return to the historical roots of the first centuries of Islam in the belief that the hegemony Islam then enjoyed would return—as can be seen in the ideas of some of the key Islamist leaders.[2]

50

Key Islamist leaders—past and current

1. Sayyid Jamal al-Din 'al-Afghani' (1838-1897)

Afghani, who came from the Indian sub-continent, aimed to transform Islam into an instrument to oppose British and Western imperialism. He could, with justification, be seen as both a precursor of attempts to modernise Islam and as providing some key concepts which later Islamists developed.

As Kramer puts it:

> In many respects, Afghani was the prototype of the modern fundamentalist. He had been deeply influenced by Western rationalism and the ideological mode of Western thought. Afghani welded a traditional religious hostility toward unbelievers to a modern critique of Western imperialism and an appeal for the unity of Islam, and while he inveighed against the West, he urged the adoption of those Western sciences and institutions that might strengthen Islam.[3]

2. Mawlana Abu al-Ala Mawdudi (1903-79)

Mawdudi was the founder of the Islamist organisation Jama'at-i Islami in British India—which became Pakistan in his lifetime. In his writings he describes the ideal Islamist state in which sovereignty would be Allah's alone, and would be exercised by a just ruler, himself guided by Allah's law. This ideological state would be administered for Allah solely by Muslim adherents of its ideology and everything would come under its sway. Kramer quotes Mawdudi thus:

> In such a state, no one can regard any field of his affairs as personal and private. Considered from this aspect the Islamic state bears a kind of resemblance to the fascist and communist states ...(and would be)... the very antithesis of secular Western democracy.[4]

Elsewhere Mawdudi writes:

> The goal of Islam is to rule the entire world and submit all of mankind to the faith of Islam. Any nation or power in this world that tries to get in the way of that goal, Islam will fight and destroy.
>
> In order for Islam to fulfil that goal, Islam can use every power available every way it can be used to bring worldwide revolution. This is *jihad*.

And:

> I don't want anybody to think that Muslims who join the party of
> God are just normal Muslim missionaries or normal preachers in the
> mosque or people who write articles. The party of God is a group
> established by Allah himself to take the truth of Islam in one hand
> and to take the sword in the other hand and destroy the kingdoms
> of evil and the kingdoms of mankind and to replace them with the
> Islamic system. This group is going to destroy the false gods and
> make Allah the only God.[5]

3. Hasan al-Banna (1906-1949)

Banna founded the Muslim Brotherhood in Egypt in 1928
largely as a reaction against the declaration of Turkey as a
secular state by Kemal Ataturk in 1924.[6]

The Muslim Brotherhood or Ikhwan in the main follows
Mawdudi's ideology. According to a very explicit website,[7]
based in California:

> Al-Ikhwan has branches in over 70 countries all over the world. The
> movement is flexible enough to allow working under the 'Ikhwan'
> name, under other names, or working according to every country's
> circumstances.

Its main objectives:

> ...are derived from the Qur'an and the tradition of the Prophet
> (pbuh)

and range from:

> 1. Building the Muslim individual;
> to
> 6. Mastering the world with Islam.

The website includes this as its theme:

> Allah is our objective.
> The messenger is our leader.
> Qur'an is our law.
> *Jihad* is our way.
> Dying in the way of Allah is our highest hope.

After Banna, the Ikhwan website names Sayyid Qutb as
its next leader and inspiration.

4. Sayyid Qutb (1903 or 1906-1966)[8]

Qutb argued that Mawdudi's Islamic state could not be
brought about by persuasion but required organisation and
force.

Qutb urged that a believing vanguard should organise itself, retreat from impious society, denounce lax Muslims as unbelievers and battle to overturn the political order. As Qutb put it: '...those who have usurped the power of God on earth and made His worshippers their slaves will not be dispossessed by dint of Word alone.' Qutb thus transformed what had been a tendency toward violence into an explicit logic of revolution.[9]

Qutb was deeply frustrated by what he called 'defeated Muslims' who distorted the meaning of *jihad* by writing about it as just a spiritual *jihad* against evil when the truth is:

Islam is nothing but Allah declaring his liberation to the human race on earth from slavery. Allah declares his lordship over the entire earth. This means that Allah greatly protests all man-made government and authorities. Absolute rebellion is a must against anything on earth that conflicts with Islam. We should eliminate and destroy with great power anything that stops Allah's revolution.[10]

Jansen has succinctly summarised the aims of Qutb and those who follow him:

A number of small fundamentalist groups have degenerated into a state of primitive rebellion. Their total lack of doubt concerning God and the Last Things is possibly to be envied, but it cohabits with murderous designs on less favoured Muslims. This desire for murder has received its theological framework from Sayyid Qutb, who was hanged in Cairo in 1966. He died with a smile on his lips. The time may be coming when citizens of the Middle East who are not willing to die smiling will have to decide whether it is worthwhile to die fighting in order to forgo the privilege of being killed by men who are ready to die smiling.[11]

5. Hassan Al Turabi (1932-)

Turabi is one of the current generation of Islamists. They studied in the West and do not want to ignore the West and all its works. Instead they want to use the strengths of the West to bring it down.

Turabi has tried to put these aims into practice in partnership with the Islamist military régime who seized power in Sudan in 1988. For Turabi, party politics:

...is a form of factionalism that can be very oppressive of individual freedom and divisive of the community, and it is, therefore, antithetical to a Muslim's ultimate responsibility to God.[12]

Turabi thus gives Islamic justification to perpetual one-party rule—the form of government he now supports and contributes to in Sudan, and which now prevails there through military force.[13]

6. *Rashid al-Ghannoushi (1941-)*

Ghannoushi also studied in the West but, on his return to Tunisia, taught the ideas of Mawdudi, Banna, and Qutb to an emerging Islamist movement. This made him unpopular with the Tunisian government and in 1989 he sought asylum in Britain where he continues to defend Islamism. His writings have recently become violently anti-semitic:

> ...declaring Jews to be the enemies not just of Islam but of all humanity, of all positive values.[14]

7. *Osama bin Laden (1957-)*

Much has been written about bin Laden and the Islamist al-Qa'eda network—including some penetrating and comprehensive studies published before September 11, 2001.[15]

He and his ideas can best be exemplified by this statement by al-Qa'eda on February 23, 1998.

> Praise be to God, who revealed the Book, controls the clouds, defeats factionalism, and says in His Book 'But when the forbidden months are past, then fight and slay the pagans wherever ye find them, seize them, beleaguer them, and lie in wait for them in every stratagem [of war]'; and peace be upon our Prophet, Mohammed Bin-'Abdullah, who said I have been sent with the sword between my hands to ensure that no one but God is worshipped, God who put my livelihood under the shadow of my spear and who inflicts humiliation and scorn on those who disobey my orders.
>
> ...'*ulema*' have throughout Islamic history unanimously agreed that the *jihad* is an individual duty if the enemy destroys the Muslim countries.
>
> On that basis, and in compliance with God's order, we issue the following *fatwa* to all Muslims.
>
> > The ruling to kill the Americans and their allies—civilians and military—is an individual duty for every Muslim who can do it in any country in which it is possible to do it, in order to liberate the al-Aqsa Mosque and the Holy Mosque [Mecca] from their grip, and in order for their armies to move out of all the lands of Islam, defeated and unable to threaten any Muslim. This is in

accordance with the words of Almighty God, 'and fight the pagans all together as they fight you all together', and 'fight them until there is no more tumult or oppression, and there prevail justice and faith in God'.

We—with God's help—call on every Muslim who believes in God and wishes to be rewarded to comply with God's order to kill the Americans and plunder their money wherever and whenever they find it. We also call on Muslim 'ulema', leaders, youths, and soldiers to launch the raid on Satan's US troops and the devil's supporters allying with them, and to displace those who are behind them so that they may learn a lesson.[16]

Kramer has summarised the Islamist ideology thus:

The idea is simple: Islam must have power in this world. It is the true religion—the religion of God—and its truth is manifest in its power. When Muslims believed, they were powerful. Their power has been lost in modern times because Islam has been abandoned by many Muslims, who have reverted to the condition that preceded God's revelation to the Prophet Mohammed. But if Muslims now return to the original Islam, they can preserve and even restore their power.

That return, to be effective, must be comprehensive; Islam provides the one and only solution to all questions in this world, from public policy to private conduct. It is not merely a religion, in the Western sense of a system of belief in God. It possesses an immutable law, revealed by God, that deals with every aspect of life, and it is an ideology, a complete system of belief about the organisation of the state and the world. This law and ideology can only be implemented through the establishment of a truly Islamic state, under the sovereignty of God. The empowerment of Islam, which is God's plan for mankind, is a sacred end. It may be pursued by any means that can be realised in terms of Islam's own code. At various times, these have included persuasion, guile, and force.[17]

Moreover, as Kramer emphasises:

What is remarkable about Islamic fundamentalism is not its diversity. It is the fact that this idea of power for Islam appeals so effectively across such a wide range of humanity, creating a world of thought that crosses all frontiers. Fundamentalists everywhere must act in narrow circumstances of time and place. But they are who they are precisely because their idea exists above all circumstances. Over nearly a century, this idea has evolved into a coherent ideology, which demonstrates a striking consistency in content and form across a wide expanse of the Muslim world.[18]

Strategy

Understandably, terrorism is currently top of the agenda. But there is substantial evidence of a concerted and coordinated strategic attack over a long period on the fundamental principles of Western societies.

Islam can provide Muslims with a religious justification for changing any existing society into an Islamic society. The aim is to make Islam supreme and to dominate every aspect of society. This is what is wanted not only by leaders like those we have just described—including Osama bin Laden—but by many Muslims all over the world according to their teaching, preaching and publications.

One example is *The Islamic Movement in the West*,[19] published in Britain in 1980 by Khuram Murad when he was head of the world-wide Islamic Foundation and a Special Advisor to General Zia ul-Haq, then President of Pakistan. Murad defines an Islamic movement as:

> ...an organised struggle to change the existing society into an Islamic society based on the Qur'an and the Sunna, and make Islam, which is a code for entire life, supreme and dominant, especially in the socio-political spheres.[20]

Murad continues:

> The idea of the Islamic movement is inherent in the very nature of Islam ... It is not necessary to give any arguments about this here but innumerable Qur'anic verses amply bear it out, like those laying down the concepts and objectives of *jihad*.[21]

Murad makes it clear that the Islamic Foundation and similar Islamic institutions are not just concerned about the immediate needs of their community:

> But it would be equally tragic if the tall and noble claims to the objective of a world-wide Islamic revolution and the ushering in of a new era are reduced to mere fulfilment of religious and educational needs. After all these needs have always been catered for in varying degrees and by various people. There was no need to launch an Islamic movement for merely meeting community needs.

> I have no hesitation in suggesting that, despite its seeming unattainability, the movement in the West should reaffirm and re-emphasise the concept of total change and supremacy of Islam in the Western society as its ultimate objective and allocate to it the highest priority.

Murad then discusses strategy, tactics, publications, and types and methods of organisation. His aims are clear and, although he writes primarily about work in Britain, they are similar to those advocated for America more than a decade later by Omar Ahmed, Chairman of the Board of CAIR (Council of American Islamic Relations):

> Islam isn't in America to be equal to any other faith, but to become dominant. The Qur'an ... should be the highest authority in America and Islam the only accepted religion on earth.[22]

Ways and Means

In 1993 Martin Kramer drew attention to the global reach of militant Islamism by identifying:

> ...the most important transformation of all: the emergence of a global village of Islamic fundamentalism.[23]

Nearly a decade later, the Internet has added considerably to the resources available to the Islamists. There are many hundreds of websites dealing with Islam in general and with Islamist organisations in particular. Islamist organisations operate across many countries around the world. It is not possible to identify more than few of them here.

Some commentators consider that the use made of the internet by some of these organisations is a dramatically new development which needs to be taken seriously.[24] The websites are used for numerous purposes which include dissemination of information about Islam, dissemination of information about specific organisations, and communication between individuals in proscribed organisations, some of which may be in the West, using both open and encrypted text.

Experienced commentators also suggest the ways in which the internet may include information gathering, possible espionage and active disruptive measures against organisations or countries which are regarded as hostile.

Organisations, websites and the internet

Al-Muhajiroun is an example of an Islamist organisation which is extremely active amongst Muslims in Great Britain. The name Al-Muhajiroun translates as the Emigrants—a reference to those who migrated with Mohammed from Mecca to Medina in 622. Their leader in the United Kingdom is Sheikh Omar Bakri Mohammed who was the founding leader of Hizb-ut-Tahrir (see below) in Britain and from which he split following differences with the Middle-East-based leadership. During 1998 Bakri Mohammed published the communiqués of Osama bin Laden for whom he claimed to act as spokesman; he has also endorsed the bombings of the United States Embassies in Dar-es-Salaam and Nairobi.[25]

Al-Muhajiroun hold numerous meetings to recruit people to their cause and they publish an extensive series of leaflets and pamphlets, both in conventional print form and on the internet.

At one such meeting a *jihad* for Chechnya was declared.[26] The meeting started with a video showing action from Dagestan and Chechnya. Multiple copies of the video were then sold to the audience for £5 upwards to help finance the *jihad* for Chechnya. Speakers at the meeting included Sheikh Omar Bakri Mohammed, a veteran fresh from Chechnya, Abu Hamza, Imam of the Finsbury Park mosque, London, and an American Imam from Chicago. The themes were hate for the Russians—and for the Americans too, although on this occasion they took second place to the Russians—and the need for urgent support for the *jihad* on the ground in Chechnya. The constant theme was 'we will win was because right is on our side and the enemy are evil. We will use the weapons and supplies of the enemy—either captured or bought—against them and defeat them in battle.'

The support sought was of three kinds: cash; public support and advocacy; and appeals to the men present to go to Chechnya to fight this *jihad* and to the women to support them.[27]

The other organisations supporting the *jihad* for Chechnya were:

- the Supporters of Shariah;
- the Committee for Defence of Legitimate Rights in Saudi Arabia;

- the International Islamic Front for *jihad* Against the Jews and Crusaders.

The Supporters of Shariah have published an article '*Jihad* in America?' on their website and have called for a *jihad* for the future of all Muslim lands with a demonstration outside the Saudi Embassy in London and a conference at the Finsbury Park Mosque[28] where the contact given was Abu Hamza.

The Committee for Defence of Legitimate Rights in Saudi Arabia was founded in Riyadh in May 1993, banned 11 days later, and transferred its headquarters to London in 1994 together with another opposition group, the Advice and Reformation Committee led by Osama bin Laden.[29]

The International Islamic Front for *jihad* Against the Jews and Crusaders is associated with Osama bin Laden and Al-Qa'eda. It has members in numerous countries, many of whom are also senior leaders in well known terrorist organisations.[30]

The style of propaganda and the manner in which meetings are conducted by Al-Muhajiroun are similar to those adopted by some Trotskyist organisations such as the Socialist Workers' Party. The emphasis is on threatening slogans, the creation of an intimidating atmosphere at meetings, the suppression of dissent and the continual switching from one issue to another as the political scene changes. The main difference is that the Islamist organisations have a religious dimension and fervour which Marxist organisations lacked.

Al-Muhajiroun: *The Voice, The Eyes And The Ears of the Muslims* (on almuhajiroun.org or ummah.org.uk) has an extensive website containing information about meetings, press releases and news items. It includes a map of the world showing alleged active bases for the organisation in Great Britain, the United States, Germany, East Africa/ Sudan, Saudi Arabia, Central Asia and Pakistan.

Under the heading About Al-Muhajiroun, the website states that:

...the following of and full implementation of ... *shari'ah* is the greatest challenge facing Muslims...

...our key goal ... [is] ...the domination of Islam World-wide;

Al-Muhajiroun's founders have been active with various Islamic movements who were and still are working to establish the Islamic state (Al-Khilafah) such as the Muslim Brotherhood (Al-Ikhwaan), Hizb ut-Tahrir, Al-Jama'at ul-Islamiyyah, Tanzeem ul-*jihad*, Young Muslims, Jamat Islami, Tableeghi Jama'ah, Young Ulama of Europe and more recently The Islamic World League.

...they do believe that *jihad* (i.e. armed struggle) is the only Islamic way to liberate the Muslim land under occupation e.g. Palestine, Kashmir, India, Chechenya and Bosnia etc;

Al-Muhajiroun's activity has quickly spread to different countries, such as: Lebanon, Saudi Arabia, Mauritius, Pakistan, Bangladesh, Afghanistan, India, Malaysia, USA, France and the UK ... and has been attacked by some governments like Egypt, Algeria, Pakistan, Saudi Arabia and Britain.

Al-Muhajiroun has many organs which are active within society under its leadership. These organs specialise in different fields such as: The Society of Muslim Lawyers, The Society of Converts to Islam, The Society of Muslim Parents, The London School of *shari'ah*, The *shari'ah* Court of The UK, The Society of Muslim Students, The Islamic World League, The Muslim Cultural Society and The Party of The Future.

Al-Muhajiroun ... [must] ... become strong and united in order to become the fifth column which is able to put pressure on the enemies of Islam ... [and so as] ... to be part of the preparations for the world-wide Islamic revolution.

Hizb-ut-Tahrir (on www.hizb-ut-tahrir.org) uses multiple languages—Arabic, English, German, Turkish and Malay—and gives details, including times and dates, of its regular meetings in the United Kingdom together with extensive literature on its aims and policies. Hizb-ut-Tahrir or the Islamic Liberation Party had its first United Kingdom-based website at Imperial College London, but following complaints to the College authorities, the site was closed down and new ones opened in their own name.[31] Hizb-ut-Tahrir were active on the campuses of universities in Britain during the early 1990s. Following representations from the National Union of Students and some other organisations, they are no longer allowed to organise or hold meetings on British campuses under the cover of 'no platform for racists' policies.[32]

More recently Hizb-ut-Tahrir has been identified as one of the key Islamist organisations threatening to destabilise many of the Central Asian Islamic republics of the former Soviet Union—Kyrgyzstan, Tajikistan, Uzbekistan, Kazakhstan and Turkmenistan as well as Pakistan.[33] Hizb-ut-Tahrir is also active in Indonesia.[34] During 2002 it has conducted poster and leaflet campaigns in London and continues to develop its internet and email campaigns.[35]

Three British members of Hizb-ut-Tahrir are currently being detained in Egypt because Hizb-ut-Tahrir is regarded there as a dangerous Islamist organisation but, as yet, it is free to operate in Britain and other Western countries.

In a recent speech in the House of Lords Baroness Cox voiced these concerns:

> Finally, there is concern about the apparent freedom of militant Islamist organisations to operate in the United Kingdom, even when they are forbidden abroad. I refer, for example, to Hizb-Ut-Tahrir. That Islamic liberation party has been described by the reputable academic Ahmed Rashid as one of the key Islamist organisations threatening to destabilise the central Asian Islamic republics as well as Pakistan. It is a proscribed organisation in Egypt and three British members are currently detained in Cairo. It is currently active in Indonesia and is distributing leaflets and conducting poster campaigns here in the United Kingdom. Its website gives details of regular meetings in this country. I ask the noble Baroness the Minister: Is that acceptable?[36]

Similar organisations with international links exist in many other Western countries. For example: Hilafet Devleti is a Turkish Islamist organisation in Germany which aims:

> ...to declare the Caliphate State of Islam, proclaim it the legitimate government of Turkey in exile and bring to an end Turkey's existing secular government.

Hilafet Devleti's published statement, *The New World Order*, says:

> Our goal is the control of Islam over everyday life. In other words, the Koran should become the constitution, the Islamic system of law should become the law and Islam should become the state ... Is it possible to combine Islam with Democracy and the layman's system on which it is based? For this question only one answer exists, and that is a resounding 'NO!'

Its leader was tried in May 2000 for incitement to murder and Joan Bakewell reported on the trial for the *New Statesman*, concluding:

> ...their followers ... exist across Europe, in Holland, Belgium, Scandinavia and Britain. Liverpool, Birmingham, Manchester and Peckham were mentioned to me. Such fanatical Islamic fundamentalists are now a threat at the heart of Europe.[37]

Nida'ul Islam (on www.islam.org.au) is another extensive website based in Sydney, Australia. It calls itself a bi-lingual comprehensive intellectual Islamic magazine, published in English and Arabic. It contains numerous news items and articles including:

- The Termination of 'Israel': A Qur'anic Fact;

- Interview with Mujahid Usamah Bin Laden—Arabian Peninsula.

The Tanzeem-e-Islami website[38] has much information, many articles and details of about a further 50 websites including those for the FIS in Algeria, the Taliban, Hizbollah, Hamas and the Muslim Brotherhood as well as Al-Muhajiroun and Hizb-ut-Tahrir.

There are also closed websites and user groups which cannot be directly accessed such as The Iconoclast[39] which claims to be providing a counter to Islamophobia in Britain.

By contrast, there are also some extensive websites which discuss Islamic matters and which are committed to conducting a reasoned debate with Islamic websites from a Christian viewpoint. These include: The Muslim-Christian Debate, and Answering Islam.[40]

In addition there are extensive websites mainly developed by former Muslims such as Faith Freedom International and The Institute for the Secularisation of Islamic Society[41] each of which raise numerous crucial issues concerning Islam and Islamism. Both of these sites include substantial lists of other similar sites.[42]

Tactics

The tactics used in the current Islamist attack on Western societies resemble those used by Marxists in the last century

—deceptions of many kinds together with the drip, feeder and multiplier effects which enhance the overall effectiveness of the committed ideologists even if their numbers are not large.

Deception

The Koran states:

> Anyone who, after accepting faith in Allah, utters unbelief—except under compulsion, his heart remaining firm in Faith, shall be absolved—but such as open their breast to unbelief—on them is wrath from Allah, and theirs will be a dreadful penalty.
>
> (Surah 16:106 [Mecca])

Shi'ite Muslims derive from this verse their doctrine of *taqiyya* which justifies conscious deception about faith for self-protection in a hostile environment. Sunni Muslims also subscribe to *taqiyya* as shown by the great Sunni writer al-Tabari's comment on this verse:

> If any one is compelled and professes unbelief with his tongue, while his heart contradicts him, to escape his enemies, no blame falls on him, because God takes his servants as their hearts believe.[43]

Thus, in extreme circumstances, deception and lying are permitted and the end justifies the means.[44]

These doctrines can clearly provide religious justification for deliberate deception—provided that the situation is perceived as threatening, which many Islamists believe is currently the case.

The doctrine could apply to those who, for example, quote a peaceful or tolerant verse from the Koran to show Islam as a religion of peace but fail to mention other verses which are warlike or intolerant.

For example, Dr Zaki Badawi, Director of the Muslim College (London) and Head of the Council of Imams and Mosques in Britain, quoted the Koran on BBC Radio 4 soon after September 11:

> We ordained that if anyone killed a person... not in retaliation of murder or in punishment... it would be as if he killed all Mankind. And if anyone saved a life it would be as if he saved the life of all Mankind.
>
> (Surah 5:32 [Medina])

He failed to mention that the very next verse reads:

> The punishment of those who wage war against Allah and His
> Messenger, and strive with might and main for mischief
> through the land is: execution, or crucifixion, or the cutting off
> of hands and feet from opposite sides, or exile from the land:
> that is their disgrace in this world, and a heavy punishment is
> theirs in the Hereafter.
>
> (Surah 5:33 [Medina])

Nor did he mention the other warlike and intolerant
verses from the Koran such as Suras 9:5, 9:29, 4:89 and 8:39
(see above).

Dr Badawi cannot be unaware of these and other provoca-
tive verses given his lifelong experience as an Islamic
scholar. Surely it is incumbent on him to explain to the
British public just what they mean and which is the true
voice of Islam.

The drip, feeder and multiplier effects

The *drip effect* refers to a stream of constant negative
criticism which gradually erodes belief in the values of
Western societies.

One relevant example of this phenomenon is the report
Islamophobia - A Challenge For Us All[45] published in 1997
which claimed to identify a new phenomenon—'Islamophobia'—which, it argued needed to be countered. A follow-
up report was published in November 2001.[46]

Unfortunately, these reports restrict themselves to
studying in depth just one society—contemporary Britain—and make virtually no effort to present evidence from
other countries or societies. This is both intellectually
dishonest and misleading since only by comparative and
balanced analysis of different kinds of society can it be seen
whether certain problems are unique or specific to a particular kind of society, or universal. And if they are not unique,
whether the problems are worse in one kind of society than
in another. To adopt such a myopic approach in the case of
Islam—which includes many different societies—is intellectually unacceptable.

These deficiencies have been highlighted very cogently in
The Westophobia Report,[47] which gives examples of quota-

tions from Muslim publications together with extensive references to sources which back up its statements. These quotations and examples show that almost all the criticisms of mainstream British society, commentators and media in the *Islamophobia* report can equally well be levied against Islamic societies. Yet there is no sign of any recognition by British Muslims that this is the case. In the *Westophobia Report*'s own words:

> Whilst British Muslims cannot be held responsible for the actions of their co-religionists overseas, they can be held accountable for their own response to Muslim harassment of Christians, especially while asserting the need for the British State and society to become more sensitive to the needs of a religious minority in their midst. If they want to avoid the accusation that this is special pleading on their part, they need to recognise their duty to uphold parallel rights for Christian minorities in Muslim states.[48]

Since many British Muslims have a continuing interest in the lands of their origin such as Pakistan, Bangladesh, Cyprus or Yemen, should there not be a clear onus on them to speak out concerning abuses of human rights in these and other Muslim states?

In 2000, a further report *Anti-Muslim Discrimination and Hostility in the United Kingdom, 2000*[49] published by the Islamic Human Rights Commission (IHRC) claimed that Muslims in Britain were being victimised by the rest of society. The report is based on a questionnaire survey. About 12,000 questionnaires were distributed but only 141 were fully completed. There is also some anecdotal evidence.

At the launch of the report[50] IHRC's chairman, Massoud Shadjareh, said:

> The levels of discrimination and the nature of anti-Muslim hostility are staggering. One is reminded of anti-Jewish hostility before the Second World War. The report's findings indicate that unless something is done urgently at a governmental level, Muslims in Britain and Europe are likely to face the same fate this century as Jews in Europe in the last.

It is difficult to reconcile the evidence given in the report with this sweeping overstatement which seems likely to inflame rather than to inform the situation.[51]

One effect of these publications is to discourage strongly any criticisms of Muslims or of Islam—either here or abroad

—while at the same time giving publicity to criticisms of Western societies.

The *feeder effect* is the policy of placing committed ideologists into key positions in society.

For example, in a recent debate in the House of Lords, Baroness Cox argued that:

> Another concern involves the financial penetration by militant Islamists of key institutions. Last year, I referred to the case of Salah Idris, the owner of a pharmaceutical factory in Sudan and therefore presumably with good relations with the Islamist NIF regime. He then owned 75 per cent of shares in the firm IES Digital Systems, which was responsible for security surveillance here in the Palace of Westminster, in British Airways and in other significant institutions. He also had a 20 per cent shareholding in Protec, a security organisation with security projects in Ministry of Defence institutions and nuclear installations at Dounreay and Sellafield. I asked the Minister whether the anti-terrorism legislation prevents the financial penetration of key institutions. To date, I have received no reply.[52]

The *multiplier effect* is the attempt to multiply the effectiveness of ideologists by the formation of front organisations whose supporters are not necessarily ideologically committed. This may include the use and misuse of charitable organisations.

One major example—currently the subject of a civil legal action in Florida—concerns Professor Sami Al-Arian of the University of South Florida. The plaintiff in the action alleges that Al-Arian has used tax-exempt charities in America such as the Islamic Concern Project (ICP) and the World Islamic Studies Enterprise (WISE) to raise money for Islamist terrorist organisations such as the Palestinian Islamic *jihad* and has received funds from another tax-exempt charity in Herndon, Virginia which was largely funded by the government of Saudi Arabia.[53]

In Britain, similar allegations about the misuse of charitable funds have been made about the worldwide World Assembly of Muslim Youth (WAMY)[54] in a programme on BBC2's *Newsnight* early in 2002.

Further evidence has been provided by Shaykh Mohammed Hisham Kabbani, chairman of the Islamic Supreme

Council of North America, to a public seminar at the State Department as long ago as January, 1999:

...there have been many non-profit organisations established in the United States whose job is only to collect money and to send it ... to extremists outside the United States. This is a big dilemma that is facing us here, because you don't know where the money is going, and it is more than hundreds of millions of dollars that have been sent to extremist parties in the Middle East and the Far East, as well as Afghanistan and the Caucasus now. Our sources say that many, many millions of dollars have been collected and sent. They send it under humanitarian aid, but it doesn't go to humanitarian aid ... some of it will go to homeless people and poor people but the majority, 90 per cent of it, will go into the black markets in these countries and buying weapon arsenals.[55]

Kabbani went on to claim that 'more than 80 per cent of the ... more than 3,000 mosques in the US' were dominated by very active extremist Islamist ideologists and that '...the extremist ideology ... is beginning to spread very quickly into the universities'.

Other examples are given by Emerson in his book *American Jihad*,[56] in which he provides evidence of links with terrorism concerning nine Muslim organisations in America: the Muslim Arab Youth Association, MAYA; The American Islamic Group, AIG; Islamic Cultural Workshop, ICW; The Council on American-Islamic Relations, CAIR; The American Muslim Council, AMC; Islamic Circle of North America, ICNA; The Muslim Public Affairs Council, MPAC; The American Muslim Alliance, AMA; and the Islamic Society of North America, ISNA. Most of these organisations are widely considered to be organisations of moderate Muslims and some have been invited to public occasions at the White House.

Six of these organisations—AMA, AMC, CAIR, MPAC, ICNA and ISNA—together with the American Muslim Political Coordination Council and the Muslim Students Association of USA and Canada combined to issue a statement which condemned Kabbani's evidence at the State Department Open Forum on Islamic extremism and demanded that he issue an apology and retraction, which he courageously declined to do.

Overall these tactics, when integrated into a coherent strategy, enable a relatively small number of people to affect and control the activities of much larger groups and organisations.

There are now many thousands of people—both in Islamic countries and in most of the free countries of the world—who are working together to further the cause of Islamism and to undermine Western societies. The preservation of the latter can therefore no longer be taken for granted and will need to be defended with wisdom, courage, understanding and sensitivity.

5

Challenges for Western Societies

Western societies must respond effectively to the challenge from ideological Islamists. To do so they need to use principles and analyses which have many parallels with the earlier conflict with ideological Marxism.

The broad distinction between terrorists operating in the name of Islam and peaceable law-abiding Muslims must be respected, but it must not be allowed to cripple the effort that is needed to preserve the principles and institutions of Western societies. At a minimum this effort requires:

- a systematic analysis of all that is said and written by ideologists and their allies;

- monitoring of Muslim organisations with documented links to Islamist activity, including the support of terrorism, identifying: who is involved, through which organisations they are working, their sources of funding and support, their main propaganda themes (anti-semitism— considerably more virulent than in National Socialist Germany—and anti-Americanism), agents of influence, front organisations, active measures and disinformation campaigns;

- scrutiny of Islamist media (MEMRI etc);

- effective publicising of this information so that the public know what is happening;

- the active recruitment of moderate Muslims in the fight against Islamic extremism;

- support for Muslims, in Western and Islamic societies, who are practising the academic mode;

- and an attempt to eliminate financial abuses of academic freedom and the other freedoms of democratic societies.

The abuse of academic freedom—the university as political base

According to Robert Fisk of the *Independent*:

> Chairs of Ottoman studies are being funded by the Turkish govern-
> ment at American universities in which US academics—who have
> to prove they have used Ottoman archives to get their jobs and thus
> must never have condemned the 1915 slaughters—propagate the lie
> that the Armenians were merely victims of 'civil war' and that Turks
> also died in the chaos of 1915. Turks did, but not on the Armenian
> scale.[1]

It is surely unacceptable for departments in universities
to accept funding under such conditions. The principles of
academic freedom by which Western universities operate
must include the requirement that all available relevant
evidence should be considered in conducting research and
arriving at conclusions. This seems clearly not to be the case
in these departments of Ottoman Studies. There may well be
other departments or units funded by sources which apply
similar restrictive conditions which abuse academic freedom.

These restrictions and conditions on funding applied to
such departments or units amount to an attempt to establish
a part of a university as a political base for a particular
faction—a tactic widely adopted by Marxists from the 1960s
onwards. This possibility merits further investigation in the
United States, in Britain and in other Western countries.
According to Professor Akbar Ahmed of Cambridge University, it is already happening at Oxford and Cambridge:

> The type of institutional base or financial backing suggests the
> intellectual position of our scholars. The Islamic Centre in Oxford
> and the Islamic Academy in Cambridge are aided by the Saudis; the
> Iranians back Siddiqui's Muslim Institute. The Saudis, we know,
> support the status quo, the Iranians support revolutionary change.
> In a sense, these institutions assume a surrogate position for the
> larger political confrontation in the Muslim world.

Ahmed goes on to quote Edward Said in support:

> It's difficult to find an intellectual who is considered to be merely a
> scholar, because everyone is associated with some tendency, some
> faction, some ideological or political line. In all Arab countries,
> academic appointments are political appointments: you have to be
> cleared.[2]

Other measures

These should include the immediate reform of immigration procedures to prevent a further influx of Islamist ideologists. Moreover, Muslims should not be given any special status that differs from that given to other religious or ethnic groups.

Western societies need not only to encourage self criticism—both of their past record and their policies for the future—but also to encourage appreciation of that record and the values and institutions of free societies. For example, Britain should:

- ensure that the Judaeo-Christian spiritual and cultural heritage is preserved and transmitted to the next generation;
- assure the teaching of Judaeo-Christian religious education, British culture and history in our schools;
- require immigrants to Britain to learn English and to respect British law.[3]

In addition, it would be helpful if more organisations could be set up which, like the International Islamic Christian Organisation for Reconciliation and Reconstruction (IICORR) mentioned in Chapter 1, seek to promote peace and mutual respect between people of different faiths and cultures. IICORR's aim is to help peaceable 'moderate' Muslims and Christians caught up in intercommunal conflict to re-establish peace, to rebuild shattered lives and communities and to establish harmonious relationships.

We will need many more such organisations and initiatives—both in this country and around the world—in the years ahead.

6

The Challenge to Islam

The Challenge for Muslims Living in the West

It is not enough for the vast majority of decent, peaceful, law-abiding Muslims to renounce terror in principle, including September 11 and similar events. They also need to renounce the view—frequently expressed by Islamists—of an inevitable war between Islam and the rest of the world. If they choose to live in Western liberal democratic societies, they must accept the values of liberal democracy—as Jews, Sikhs, Hindus and others have done for many years.

Moderate Muslims also need to take a stand on other issues such as:

- slavery, including its modern manifestations in the Muslim world;
- human rights abuses wherever they occur including those concerning religious freedom, freedom of speech, and equality of opportunity for women.

Many Muslims are quick to criticise any non-Muslims who raise these thorny issues. For example, Lord Ahmed speaking in the House of Lords in November, 1999 said that extremist Islamist behaviour was not typical and that the active members of Al-Muhajiroun made up no more than about 0.1 per cent of the Muslim population. However, if this estimate is accurate, it still represents some thousands of people in Britain whose ideological commitment embraces subversive or terrorist activities.

The kind of special pleading identified in the report of the Islamic Human Rights Commission makes no attempt to present a balanced view of the situation. It ignores the situation of Christians or Jews within contemporary Islamic societies—a major omission in any serious discussion of human rights.

Should Muslims not acknowledge that in Western societies they are better protected, more prosperous but above all more free—to speak, to publish, to vote and to exercise numerous other freedoms—than they would be in almost any Islamic country?

And should they also not acknowledge that there are few Muslim countries that offer Christians, Jews or those of other religions the freedom to practice their religion that Muslims enjoy in Western societies? And should they not work to redress this asymmetry and to promote religious and other freedoms in Islamic countries?

Some recent examples from the 1980s and 1990s in the Muslim world are illuminating. Writers in particular have been under threat. The courageous and outspoken Egyptian writer Farag Foda was murdered, and some Islamist preachers justified the assassination by declaring him an apostate.

According to Duran, other writers:

> ... have been assassinated or threatened with assassination in Afghanistan, Algeria, Iran, Kuwait, Lebanon, Pakistan, Syria, Turkey, Yemen, and the Western Diaspora, including the United States. Few safe havens remain.

> The Battle of the Books raging in much of the Arab and Muslim world leads to the questions of how much freedom intellectuals can exercise without risking their lives, how much independent thinking is allowed, and what opportunities there are to express opinions freely. In short, is a Muslim Enlightenment possible?

> ... Many members of the Muslim world's intellectual élite now live in North America and Western Europe. Until his death in 1988, their leader was Fadlu-r-Rahman, professor of Islamic Studies at the University of Chicago ... in 1969 he was forced to leave his native Pakistan because of a book published in Britain. Candidates for the Nobel Prize in literature live in Europe; the Moroccans Idris Shara'ibi (Driss Chraibi) and Tahir Bin Jillun (Tahar Ben Jelloun) in France, and the Sudanese At-Tayyib Salih in Britain—one of his books was banned by the Islamist dictatorship in his native country.[1]

The need for reform is however recognised by some leading Muslims such as Tariq Ali, the Pakistani intellectual who had been a Marxist revolutionary in the 1960s:

We are in desperate need of an Islamic Reformation that sweeps away the crazed conservatism and backwardness of the fundamentalists but, more than that, opens up the world of Islam to new ideas which are seen to be more advanced than what is currently on offer from the West. This would necessitate a rigid separation of state and mosque; the dissolution of the clergy; the assertion by Muslim intellectuals of their right to interpret the texts that are the collective property of Islamic culture as a whole; the freedom to think freely and rationally and the freedom of imagination. Unless we move in this direction we will be doomed to re-living old battles, and thinking not of a richer and humane future, but of how we can move from the present to the past. It is an unacceptable vision.[2]

A problem for moderate Muslims?

We have drawn a distinction between the vast majority of moderate Muslims and ideological Islamists. But the distinction depends in practice on moderate Muslims being more forthright in distinguishing themselves from their ideological co-religionists.

There seems to be considerable reluctance for them to make the necessary distinctions—a reluctance which is apparent both within Western societies and within Islamic societies. It seems to be extremely difficult for most moderate Muslims to take up any public positions against those of the ideological Islamists and to retain credibility within their own communities.

The question therefore arises as to whether there is any fundamental reason within Islam for this reluctance to take issue with extremism, especially in public.

John Habgood, the former Archbishop of York, in his recent book *Varieties of Unbelief*, discusses this topic:

I base my remarks on the work of a Muslim anthropologist, Akbar Ahmed, now a professor in Cambridge, who a few years ago wrote a much acclaimed book on *Postmodernism and Islam*...

...In theory he welcomes the possibility of diverse people and cultures learning from one another, but his emphasis is almost entirely on the confrontation between Islam and the Western culture responsible, as he sees it, for postmodernist excesses. He writes passionately about the Muslim sense of being beleaguered and misunderstood, and about the destructive force of the media. But there is almost no acknowledgement that there are common intellectual problems facing all religion, and that the intellectual content of Islam itself might be under threat. This absence of concern is linked with what was to me one of his most surprising disclosures. He describes how after the great period of intellectual dominance when Islamic scholars had preserved Greek philosophy for medieval Europe, Islam virtually rejected its Greek heritage and with it the spirit of criticism. He then adds, 'This rejection may help to explain the deep-rooted cultural and intellectual opposition to Islam in the West *where the ancient Greek still matters*.'[3] The West, in other words, is blamed for wanting to learn from the Greeks about how to be rational. From the contrasted viewpoint of a Christian historian, the Muslim withdrawal from the intellectual ferment of medieval Europe is seen as a disaster for Islam. It lay in 'the sharp dichotomy between reason and will that characterises the Qur'an's doctrine of the Creator'.[4] If God's will is all we need to know, mere thinking can become impious.

These two characteristics of Islam, its sense of disorientation in the encounter with a social and political system it does not control, and its distrust of the tradition of rational religious criticism, are potential sources of weakness, just as they are for those forms of Christianity which share with Islam a desire to distance themselves from secular society and to rely on exclusive possession of an infallible written guide. Professor Ahmed has a perceptive analysis of the different ways in which Muslims react in an alien culture and of the dangers of retreating into anger and extremism. He is aware of the difficulties Muslims face in participating in a global civilisation without losing their identity. But just as on the one hand Christians may fail to integrate their faith into the patterns of social life, so on the other hand Muslims seem not to have grasped the significance of the necessary and inbuilt tension between religious faith and any actual social order. Quite the contrary. But unless there is also a critical element in that relationship, a critical element which for Christians is centred on the cross of Christ, the almost inevitable result is some form of absolutism through the alliance of political and religious power. It is a lesson which the Christian churches have had to learn, often painfully, but which is clearly at present much more difficult for Islam.

The fact that the Qur'an is beyond criticism only compounds the problem. The internal strength of Islam is gained at the cost of not being able openly to examine its own foundations. There is, of course, an internal logic in saying that if God is truly God then no critical examination of his revelation is possible. But it is a logic which, if pursued, cuts Islam off from any meaningful dialogue either with other faiths, or even within itself, and makes the Qur'an's own claim that it is the fulfilment of all religion viciously circular.[5]

This perceptive analysis poses further questions which need to be discussed openly by moderate Muslims in order to reassure non-Muslims, prevent the growth of Islamophobia and to enhance the appreciation of the valuable contributions made in so many fields by many Muslims.

Summary

1. Definitions and Distinctions

- Since September 11 and similar terrorist acts by 'Islamic' groups, there is a risk of Islamophobia and a backlash against all Muslims, including the vast majority who are peaceable, law-abiding citizens.

- There is also a growing interest in Islam, with many non-Muslims studying Islamic history, writings and contemporary practices; inevitably, comparisons will be made with Western societies.

- Though Western societies are heterogeneous, in modern times such societies have generally shared the fundamental beliefs, values, and institutions of liberal democracy—with obvious exceptions, such as the National Socialism of Nazi Germany. But there are enough common elements for comparison.

- 'Islamic' societies encompass an even greater heterogeneity, ranging from those with secular constitutions and some of the political institutions of liberal democracies (Turkey, Indonesia) to those based on more traditional Islamic values (Saudi Arabia) or committed to Islamist beliefs and practices (Afghanistan under the Taliban). 'Islamism' and 'Islamist' are the terms now widely used to refer to radical, militantly ideological versions of Islam—as defined by the practitioners themselves—suffused with religious justifications for violent or revolutionary political action. By 'traditional Islam' we mean the Islamic doctrines developed from the seventh up to about the ninth century. Since 'Islamists' frequently claim allegiance to these doctrines it is sometimes appropriate to consider traditional Islam and Islamism together.

- Islamic societies and militant Islamism need to be distinguished since a hostile response to Islamist terrorism could quickly become hostility to all Muslims. It is our hope and intention in writing this paper that non-Muslims may develop a better understanding of Islam and better relationships with moderate peaceable Muslims, and that both Muslims and non-Muslims may thus develop appropriate responses to the current complex situation.

2. Comparisons

We compare Western societies with Islamic societies at two levels.

(i) The most fundamental level involves concepts of knowledge and truth and the kinds of institutions needed to promote and preserve them.

- In Western societies truth about any subject is sought, in universities and elsewhere, by experts who use all available evidence, logical argument, public debate and criticism to arrive at their always provisional conclusions. These conclusions—and the tentative ethos which created them—are transmitted to the next generation through education. One aim is to produce autonomous individuals who can think for themselves, in a spirit of academic criticism and self-criticism.

- In traditional Islamic and Islamist societies truth is the word of Allah as revealed to his Prophet Mohammed and recorded in the Koran together with the sayings and actions of the Prophet as recorded in the *hadith* and *sunnah*. This is interpreted and transmitted during education and later by the *'ulema'*—the experts in these matters. The aim is to produce truly Islamic devout Muslims. One result is some inhibition of critical free individual enquiry.

- These radically different epistemological and philosophical approaches to the concepts of truth and knowledge underpin and shape the very different social and political structures in Western societies, compared with traditional Islamic and Islamist societies.

(ii) Social, Political, Legal and Economic Institutions.

- Modern Western societies are ideally based on the values of tolerance, pluralism and individual freedoms in political, economic, cultural, educational and religious institutions and, most crucially, in the institutions concerned with freedom of expression, communication and access to information. Like their universities, Western societies are relatively decentralised. Although Western societies are not immune from corruption, their institutions and values help to provide complex checks and balances on the exercise of power.

- Traditional Islamic and Islamist societies tend to be monolithic and dictatorial, intolerant of dissent, and lacking in individual freedoms. There tends to be more control over all aspects of life—legal, political, economic, cultural, educational, religious—which is frequently exercised in the name of Islam. Freedom of expression and of access to information are often limited and few if any effective checks exist on the exercise of power by the ruling or governing group.

- Two central concepts from traditional Islam—*shari'a and jihad* (Islamic Holy Law and Islamic Holy War or struggle)—have been revived and extended by modern Islamists in ways which are incompatible with the United Nations Universal Declaration of Human Rights, especially with regard to equality before the law and equality between men and women.

- The *shari'a* is derived from the Koran and the *hadith*; there is no other kind of Islamic law. *Shari'a* law requires inequalities between Muslims and: (i) Christians/Jews; (ii) all other non-Muslims; and also between men and women. Slavery has been endemic in the Muslim world for centuries and still continues in, for example, Sudan today.

- *Jihad* can be interpreted spiritually as a struggle to lead a holy life. But it can be extended to mean an obligation—imposed by Allah on all Muslims—to strive unceasingly to convert or to subjugate non-Muslims. *Jihad* in this latter sense is without limit of time or space and continues until the whole world accepts Islam or submits to the Islamic state.

- Western societies vary in the extent to which they are based on the values of a free market economy or socialist values with more centralised economies. However, there are common features associated with capitalist economic systems. They may show problems such as unacceptable economic inequalities, financial corruption and excessive promotion of materialistic values. However, capitalism, despite these problems, has proved a highly successful wealth-generating economic system, which has tended to promote improved standards of living for citizens living in capitalist societies.

• Many Islamic societies have limited economic freedom and limited economic success compared with many non-Muslim countries; and they tend to be dependent on the import of science and technology from the West.

The fundamental conflict between modern Western societies and modern Islamism is documented by discussing the writings of key Islamists, past and present, including Osama bin Laden; discussing the strategy and tactics adopted by Islamists: and giving documented examples of these world-wide activities including evidence of the extensive use made of international organisations, websites and the internet.

The evidence presented raises many fundamental questions and challenges for both Muslims and non-Muslims as to how militant Islamism can be effectively resisted and as to whether Islam in its present forms is compatible with liberal democracy.

Conclusion

Every effort has been made to ensure that these comparisons and analyses, although inevitably oversimplified, are accurate and objective.

• It is not our intention to suggest that 'West is Best'— Western societies are beset by numerous social and economic problems, and by many personal crises of beliefs and values.

• However, as non-Muslims are beginning to study Islam in order to try to understand its role in the modern world, many will inevitably make comparisons with their own societies and encounter the kinds of questions we have had to face, as we have sought to understand Islam in the world today—through reading scholarly books and Muslims' own writings and websites and through encountering conflict zones such as Sudan, Nigeria, the Caucasus and Indonesia.

- It is our hope that Muslims will be able to respond sympathetically and to address these and other complex issues in ways which will increase mutual understanding between Muslims and those of other faiths, decrease the threat of Islamophobia and facilitate the mutual respect, appreciation and co-existence needed for the survival of these contemporary civilisations.

Appendix
Contemporary Case Studies

When it happens to you, you'll know it's true

Russian proverb quoted by Alexander Solzhenitsyn

Introduction

A. Slavery in Sudan:
   Case Study 1 Testimony of former slaves
   from Mayen Abun, Bahar-El-Ghazal

   1. A lady with bandage on her face, aged about 38

   2. A boy aged 13 from Mayen Abun

   3. Interview with Arab slave traders

   Case Study 2 Mende Nazer's Story:
   A slave in Sudan and in London

B. Military Offensives Against Civilians:
   Jihad and Forced Conversion
   Case Study 3 Military offensive against civilians:
   Sudan, June 2002

   Case Study 4 Military offensives combined,
   in some cases, with forced conversion to Islam:
   Indonesia, 2000

   Interview with a young man aged 17,
   from Lata-Lata island in Bacan Group, North Maluku.

Introduction

Much of the discussion in this paper has focused on the essential beliefs and values underpinning Islamic policies and practices throughout history. They show a degree of consistency over time and in different parts of the world, despite the variations in historical contexts and pre-existing cultures.

Moreover, many of the published studies of Islam draw their examples from historical evidence. But in various parts of the world, traditional Islamic practices associated with the more militant interpretation of the concept of *jihad* persist, including military offensives against innocent civilians, slavery and forced conversion to Islam.

We offer some examples based on first-hand evidence, both to illustrate the reality of these policies and to encourage Muslims to explain their response to these situations which represent serious violations of human rights, as embodied in the Universal Declaration of Human Rights. This would be very helpful, as many of these practices are occurring in countries which are signatories to the Universal Declaration, and those who are concerned with violations of human rights must challenge them wherever they occur. Therefore, reassurances by Muslims would be timely and help to prevent negative perceptions of Islam which, as we have argued earlier, may promote the growth of Islamophobia.

A. Slavery in Sudan

Much has been written about the widespread practice of slavery in Africa. A number of the studies have focused on 'traditional' practices of slavery carried out by Africans themselves as part of inter-tribal conflicts. There have also been a great number of studies of the slave trade, perpetrated mainly by European traders, purchasing many millions of Africans and deporting them under brutal conditions across the Atlantic to a fate of slavery in the plantations and servitude in the New World.[1] This form of slavery has also been depicted and decried in many other ways, including exhibitions, novels and exhibitions. It has become an indelible part of the record of the role played by

European colonisers in African history, and it has been widely and rightly condemned.

John Azumah's book[2] is one among many which provide authoritative accounts of the long-standing tradition of slavery in this part of Africa. But, while recognising both the existence of forms of 'traditional' slavery amongst African tribes and communities and the systematic transatlantic slave trade, he highlights the relatively under-researched and unpublicised forms of Arab-African slavery. He documents in chilling detail the massive enslavement of Africans by Arabs, and his studies suggest a conservative estimate of between 11 and 14 million Africans taken into servitude in Muslim lands, outside tropical Africa, over 14 centuries.

This practice continues today, for example, in Sudan. Human rights and humanitarian aid activists working in areas such as Bahr-El-Ghazal and the Nuba Mountains have encountered large numbers of Africans who have suffered as a result of slavery encouraged by the current National Islamic Front (NIF) 'Government of Sudan'.

This régime took power by military coup in 1989 and retains it by military force, despite massive political and armed confrontation by many opposition movements —African and Arab, Muslim as well as Christian and adherents of traditional religion. After seizing power, the NIF declared *jihad* against all who oppose it. The weapons of its *jihad* include military offensives against innocent civilians; the manipulation of humanitarian aid; and slavery. Every month the NIF publishes a list of areas which are 'open' to the United Nations Operation Lifeline Sudan (UNOLS) and humanitarian organisations working under its aegis—and those which are 'closed'. Typically, it will undertake its massive military offensives in areas it designates 'closed', so no-one will visit them to take humanitarian aid to the victims or to witness what has happened. Such raids involve wholesale slaughter of civilians—men, women and children—and the total destruction of communities through scorched-earth policies. In areas such as Bahr-El-Ghazal, the tendency is to kill most of the men and to abduct women and children into slavery.

Due to the frequent designation by the NIF of such areas as 'closed', most major aid organisations will not visit them and obtain the evidence of the effects of this *jihad*. However, some organisations are prepared to risk going to 'No Go' areas in order to take essential humanitarian aid and to obtain the evidence of the NIF's violations of human rights.

Some organisations such as Swiss-based Christian Solidarity International (CSI) and the derivative organisation Christian Solidarity Worldwide (CSW) have visited locations in these areas on many occasions, often accompanied by independent media representatives. They have met many hundreds of women and children who have been enslaved and the leaders of the local communities who have given detailed evidence of the NIF's policies with regard to slavery. They have also taken evidence from Arab Muslim traders from the north who describe the NIF's policy from their own experience.

The combined evidence obtained from many visits and numerous interviews since 1995 can be summarised. In essence, as the NIF escalated its *jihad*, it began to promote slavery as one of the weapons of war and as an ideal method of achieving three of the objectives of *jihad*: destruction of African communities and culture; forced Islamisation of those not already Muslims; and forced Arabisation of Africans.

In the early 1990s, leading NIF figures visited borderland areas such as those in Southern Kordofan and Darfur; mobilised the local Arab tribesmen; encouraged them to participate in the *jihad*; regretted they could not pay money but promised them the right to keep the bounty of war as their reward—including the human bounty as slaves; legitimated the practice of enslavement, assuring them that it is justified in the Koran, as part of *jihad*, as a means of conversion to Islam; and provided logistical back-up on 'slave raids' with provision of horses, weapons (e.g. AK 37 rifles) and additional troops from government regular army forces and Popular Defence Front (PDF) mujahadeen warriors.

The resulting raids were so massive that there was nothing the local African, mainly Dinka, peoples could provide as effective resistance, armed only with their traditional spears.

On the first visit undertaken by one of the authors, Caroline Cox, after this new policy was initiated, to Nyamllel in Bahr-El-Ghazal, 80 men and two women had been killed (their bodies were in a mass grave) and 282 women and children had been abducted into slavery.

Many subsequent visits to locations which have suffered slave raids have provided the opportunity to meet and to interview recently returned slaves. Their accounts of their enslavement are highly convincing: systematic, consistent and often corroborated by visible evidence of physical abuse.

These two examples illustrate the kind of conditions women and children typically have to endure as slaves. A great deal of evidence has been collected over several years. This has been associated with the policy of slave redemption undertaken by organisations such as CSI and CSW. This policy has been seen as controversial and has attracted considerable criticism. CSW has justified its involvement in redemption and has responded to its critics (see Section C below).

On many occasions, independent television, radio and newspaper reporters have accompanied visits in which slaves have been redeemed. Most set out deeply sceptical or overtly critical. After interviewing the ex-slaves, they returned convinced of the reality of slavery in Sudan today (see, for example, the BBC 'Everyman' TV programme, 29 January 2001).

Case Study 1
Slavery: Testimony of former slaves from Mayen Abun, Bahar-El -Ghazal[3]

Many visits to Sudan have resulted in scores of detailed interviews with former slaves and the Arab traders who bring them back to freedom. These three examples are typical and can be multiplied many times. They show a consistency which is convincing and the evidence of their suffering is compelling.

1. A lady with bandage on her face, aged about 38

The armed raiders came to her village on horseback. She was captured with her three children and forced to walk for ten days. There were more than one thousand people captured from different areas. They were fed left-overs such as bones and a cup of water or tea; they were not allowed sufficient water to drink. They took the leaves of the tamil tree to get water. They were tied together in groups at night whilst they slept. They were driven north to Chatap village near Abyie and then divided into groups and ordered to fetch water, grind grain or tend the goats/donkeys. They were given Arabic names: she was named Amuna, the children were named Mohamed, Abdullah, Adam, Soloman and Abdollei. They were forced to observe Islamic practices such as attending the mosque; when they refused, they were beaten. The woman conceived a child by her owner.

The children were separated from their brothers and sisters. One of the boys worked for an owner called Mohammed in Chatap village. He was responsible for looking after his master's animals from 6 a.m. to 6 p.m. He was given left-overs of food to eat and was not given bread, even though his master had bread, and had to sleep on the floor without even a groundsheet or mosquito net. His master had four children of his own but treated him as a servant, as did the children. He never saw his sister during his time in captivity as they had been separated and they were in a different area. He was beaten by his master. He was told by his master to attend the mosque but refused because he was a Catholic and didn't want to become a Muslim.

2. A boy aged 13 from Mayen Abun

In February 1998, Malek was looking after his cattle when about 25 armed raiders came to the village, ten were on horseback, the remainder on foot. They took him along with the 20 cows that he was tending. His father was killed by the raiders and his mother and brothers and sisters were taken captive (his mother, three brothers and five sisters remain in Chatap). When Malek refused to go with them, they beat him and took him to where they were holding the others. They were tied together and forced to walk for ten days to Chatap. There were more than one thousand women and children in this group and some died from hunger during the journey. His master's name was Mohammed Abduli. He was given the name Mohammed and they forced him to attend the mosque. He tried to run away from the mosque many time but was beaten. He finally managed to escape whilst tending the cattle. It took him ten days to walk to Abyei; he survived by eating fruit and gum. In Abyei he found people to work for, in return for food. From Abyei he met up with others who were heading south. He reached Mayen Abun in July 1999. He is very worried that the raiders might come again and has regular nightmares.

3. Interview with Arab slave traders

There are few men amongst the slaves because they have been killed or conscripted into the military. If a man refuses he is liable to be killed. The Arab traders claimed that, under *shari'a* law, they are permitted to capture the children or families of the people they are fighting. The traders stated that the government in Khartoum is contributing artillery, rifles and ammunition so that they can clear the Dinkas off their land and graze their own cattle there. During the raids Mujahideen are joined by government forces to attack the Dinkas. One of the traders stated that he had taken part in 21 such raids. The traders confirmed that captured slaves are sold to other Arab countries but could not confirm to which countries they were taken.

Case Study 2
Mende Nazer's Story: A slave in the Sudan and in London

Mende Nazer is a Sudanese Muslim who was enslaved first in Sudan and then in London. She has published a best-selling book in Germany[4] that describes how she was kidnapped in a slave raid in the Nuba mountains of Sudan when she was around 12 years old and then sold into slavery. After spending eight years enslaved to a rich Arab family in Khartoum, she was then brought to London by a senior Sudanese diplomat. She escaped that diplomat's household and claimed asylum in the UK in September 2000. Whilst in slavery, Ms Nazer suffered horrific abuses including beatings and sexual assaults. This is how she describes her story:

> I always dreamed of becoming a doctor, so I worked hard at school and was encouraged by my family in Karko in the Nuba mountains. On the day of the raid, we came out of the hut to see armed men on horseback going through the village, torching all the huts and killing and beating. It was complete chaos. In the confusion I let go of my father's hand and we lost each other. The next thing I was taken by the hand by a man who smiled at me and led me away. I assumed he was trying to take me away to safety.

> With other children, I was taken on horseback to Dilling and then by truck to Khartoum. I was taken by a woman—some years later I heard her tell a visitor she had paid a lot of money for me.

> The house seemed like a palace to me. I worked seven days a week without a break and my hours were from 7 a.m. to very last thing at night. I was very badly treated for six to seven years.

> My mistress regularly slapped me across the face with her hands or a wooden-soled shoe. At night she locked me up in a shed.

> In 2000 she told me I would be sent to work in London. She instructed me exactly what to say to embassy officials.

> I was told to say I was treated well ... [the lady] was much kinder to me in that she did not beat me. But I had to work very hard looking after the house and five children. She retained my passport. I was not allowed to leave the house alone apart from to take rubbish to the bin. I was not paid anything, ever. I was depressed and desperate.

B. Military Offensives Against Civilians: Jihad and Forced Conversion

Contemporary examples of the continuation of this practice can be found in may parts of the world, including Sudan, northern Nigeria and Indonesia.

In all these countries, Muslims and Christians had traditionally lived peaceably together, often intermarrying and sharing communal festivals and family celebrations. But the rise of militant Islamism has been associated with the development of armed conflicts, often involving foreign mercenaries and sophisticated weapons brought in from abroad.

Case Study 3
Military offensive against civilians: Sudan, June 2002

These case studies are based on interviews with a group of internally displaced Mabaan people from villages which were attacked by Government of Sudan forces in early May, 2002. They had fled from their villages, Yawaji, Kawaji and Dengaji, in Eastern Upper Nile.

1. A woman named Nyanyaul Moon who lived in Yawaji said that she had lived there since childhood and had married there so it had always been her home. On the morning of the attacks, soldiers came early in the morning; they were wearing uniforms and came in trucks with guns and heavy weapons. They were firing their guns and burned homes and crops. People did not expect an attack and some of those who did not realise in time what was happening, failed to escape and were killed. On the first day of the attack 27 people were killed, including women and children. Everyone else fled and Nyanyaul Moon did not know what happened to those who fled in different directions—she did not even know if they were still alive.

The soldiers took everything: cooking pots, clothes, mosquito nets. But, above all, she lost nine children—four boys and five girls. She is now alone without anybody to take care of her. The men tried to defend the area with farm implements, mainly axes and machetes, but there were too many NIF troops so that they were overwhelmed. The attackers came to kill, to destroy and to plunder. She has also lost her younger brother who disappeared and was not found among the dead. She does not know what happened to him.

2. A woman named Yowa Wale. Her five children and her sister's five children were killed during that morning attack:

> We ran—we do not know where. We do not know where we can settle and live because we have lost our family and everything. We had to

flee and after the attack we found that everything was burnt. We ran and ran to save our lives just seeking to find a place where we could survive. After we escaped, because we had nothing, we became ill on the way. There was no treatment available and we do not what to do. Because we have to find somewhere to settle, we came here because we heard there might be some help—medicine and food, but there is nothing here.

My husband was there but I have not seen him since I fled. My five children were aged between seven and eighteen; they were members of our church congregation but I have no idea where they are.

3. A man named Ginar Thekie from Yawaji:

When the NIF troops came to the village they saw that we had blankets and supplies, so they tried to take everything, looting, burning, leaving us with nothing. This was only a village of civilians—there was no army here. We have been left with nothing. Many people never arrived here, because they died on the way because there was no water or food. Therefore we do not know where they are or even if they are still alive. Some were killed by the guns, others from hunger and thirst. Therefore we just sit here and we do not know what to do. We have nothing—no homes, no medicines, and some are ill. I have lost three children and do not know where they are. Another of my children, aged about eight, was burnt inside our hut. His body was found when some men went back to see what had happened.

Case Study 4
Military offensives combined, in some cases, with forced conversion to Islam: Indonesia, 2000

The objectives of these military offensives include the killing of non-Muslims and moderate Muslims who oppose the militants. In some cases, moderate Muslims have died alongside Christians, helping them to defend their churches and communities against attacks by militants such as the forces of the Lasker *jihad* movement which undertook many attacks on Christian communities in the Moluccas and in Central Sulawesi. They numbered several thousand *jihad* warriors, many of whom were known to have come from abroad.

While the majority of attacks focused on the killing of local people and the destruction of their communities, some also involved attempts to enforce conversion to Islam through threatening captives with death—giving them the choice of 'surrender by sword or surrender by conversion'.

One example illustrates all these aspects of contemporary military *jihad* in Indonesia:

Interview with a young man aged 17, from Lata-Lata island in Bacan Group, North Maluku.

In February 2000, my village (I was then 15 years old) was attacked. The assault was unexpected, as our people had had no problems with Muslims. Just before it happened, one person warned us, but we didn't believe him; we thought it was a provocation, so we continued fishing in the sea and working in our fields.

At 1 p.m. two ships arrived and shouted that in a moment they would land and wipe us out, so we then alerted everyone we could. But the people could not prepare to defend themselves as we had no weapons.

At 3 p.m. the attack began. Apart from those coming from the boats (there were about a hundred men in each of the bigger boats and several smaller boats with about ten people in each) many others came from the jungle, over the mountains—it seemed as if they were about 5,000 (but it is impossible to tell). The men who came in the boats wore long white gowns; those from the jungle wore short white tunics.

They began bombing from the jungle and shooting from the boats. There were about 1,700 people in our community and we had nothing to defend ourselves with. We were overwhelmed. About 70 of our people were killed. There was nothing we could do, so those who could, fled into the jungle. Those who were killed were those who could not run—mainly the elderly, women and children. I saw my grandmother running into the ocean; they speared her, seven other of my relations were killed: one had his head sliced off above the eyes; another was decapitated through the mouth. When we returned later to see what had happened, I saw one of my cousins, aged seven, had been beheaded.

Another villager described how someone had been impaled on a pole and how, as the attack developed, and as we fled, he saw military men wearing white gowns, shooting his uncle, pouring fuel over him and setting him alight.

At 5 p.m., with the Head of the village, we fled inland. By then, there was no-one alive in the village. The head of the village took me with him. We walked for about an hour and then sat and prayed for God's protection. When the Lasker *jihad* had attacked the village they had kept shouting: 'Why do you Christians believe in Christ? Why believe in that long-haired man?'

As we were running, they had shouted: 'Kill the Head of the village and the Pastor. They are provocateurs and terrorists. We must kill them.'

We hid in the jungle. All we had to eat were coconuts and plants. Water was such a problem that people drank from muddy puddles.

Next morning, we looked at the village and saw what had happened to our families. We were very confused and didn't know what to do. It is a small island and our boats had been destroyed. Everything had been destroyed. We didn't know where to go. We had nowhere to escape. We started to bury the dead, but at 7 a.m. the Laser *jihad* returned, shouting: 'Why touch those heathen?'

We realised we couldn't escape from the island and we knew that if we were caught we would be asked: 'Do you wish to surrender by religion (convert to Islam) or by war (be killed)?'

They sent messengers to the villagers still hiding in the jungle, saying that if the pastor did not surrender himself, within three days, they would go through the island and kill everyone on the island. They also gave orders that everyone in hiding must come out and surrender or they would be hunted down and killed.

Those of us in my group in the jungle talked and agreed we would convert to Islam with our bodies—otherwise we would all be killed. But in our hearts we would not convert. When we came out of the jungle, we found that others who had already surrendered had been circumcised, including women and girls from the age of seven.

When I was asked by the military men why I had run away, I said I believed in Christ. They said: 'Christianity is not a true religion. Why do you just sing and laugh and not bow down before God?'

I could do nothing except obey them. I was also circumcised.[5]

I saw them capture the pastor (Pastor Patissina) on Goji beach. They bound his hands and feet tightly together. He said he was thirsty and one Lasker *jihad* solider (named Baha from Bokimaki) retorted: 'We are going to leave you like this until you die.'

The young man to whom we were talking thought Baha was with military troops from Java, possibly a unit from East Java. Also present on the beach were religious leaders, officials from political parties, including Ustad Agus Wahid (secretary of the Keadilan party in Jakarta—a small party in the national parliament). Also present during the signing of the conversion statement were Ustud Kasuba, a convert to Islam and chairman of the Keadilan party in Ternate and a Dr Taufik from Ternate who, together with Ustud Agus, later transported those who were recruited to Jakarta.

Others who were present at the 'celebration feast' following the circumcisions were the head of the police sector Kapolsek, a military commander Danramil, the District Mayor Camat and other government officials from Ternate. They were all celebrating the conversion of 1,700 Christians to Islam.

He was told that they eventually shot the Pastor and took his body to the island of Sidanga where they hung it up for public display. Also, four elders of the church were killed alongside the Pastor and their bodies were said to have been taken to Sidanga and left to be eaten by dogs. It was reported that they had all been tortured before being killed— finger and toe nails had been pulled out and their bodies were cut by machetes in many different parts. Although payment was made for their bodies, all that could be found were mangled remains.

Ustad Agus from Jakarta, who had led the people making their statements of forced conversion ('There is no God but Allah' and 'Mohammed is his Prophet'), asked some parents if he could take their young people away to Jakarta for training. They agreed, thinking there might be some chance for them to escape.

I was recruited and subjected to many, many questions about what I believed, why Christians sing songs and worship as we do. I was mocked about how my God could die and live again and told that Christians tell lies. I tried to take my Bible with me, but it was taken from me and burnt. Also my pictures of Christ were taken from me and I was told I would be taken 'to the land of the Arabs'.

Four young people were taken and we were given new non-Christian names. On 1 March 2000, we were taken to Jakarta to be sent to passandrin (religious schools). I was taken to one in West Java in Indramayu (he estimates it is about two hours by bus from Jakarta).

In school, I was taught that Christianity is false: the only true faith is Islam and Mohammed is the only true Prophet. We were trained to become Lasker *jihad* warriors and were allocated to a group to be sent to fight in Maluku. I said I did not want to go to Maluku but I was told by Jaffa Umar Talib that I had to train to become a real servant of God and any *jihad* is good experience and that if we went to fight on a *jihad*, when we die, we would be served by 72 'fairy women' who would take care of our sexual needs.

I was allowed to stay for 'further training' instead of being sent to Maluku. However, after September 11, in order to prove my commitment to 'the cause', I was required to join demonstrations in Jakarta. I was given an American flag and ordered to burn it and to join in protests against America as a terrorist nation.

I subsequently had to support the cause of Osama Bin Laden and register to go to fight in Afghanistan. I was told that 10,000 had already registered and that the person behind the mobilisation was Amien Reis.

When we gathered for the meeting of those going to Afghanistan, Amien Reis told us that on a *jihad* we should not kill women and children. But one person protested that if we did not kill women and children, we would 'leave a seed behind for them to grow'. Amien Reis then said 'It is up to you what you do'.

When I returned to the passandrin, I prayed not to have to go. Then it was decided that the students at our passandrin would not be sent, because we were younger and could be left to continue our study.

We were told that Maluku was 'still in the process of becoming an Islamic State'. I therefore realised there might be some hope that it had not been conquered and my parents might still be alright.

We were taught to hate the heathen kaffirs and that in due course we would be sent to Maluku to teach the people to submit to God—or to train forces who would make them submit. I therefore wondered if it really was safe in Maluku. In my room I prayed very hard and the next day I received a message from a friend that the people in my village had fled and returned to Christianity.

I received a telephone call from my brother who tried to send me a signal that he would help me to escape. He asked for my address but I couldn't give it because my *kiai* (Islamic teacher) was standing next to me. Eventually my brother managed to ring when I was alone and I gave details. One day when the guards were away, he arrived and pretended to be a Muslim, he collected me.

Notes

Foreword

1   Acton, J., *The History of Freedom and Other Essays*, London: Macmillan, 1907, p. 52.

1: A Comparison between 'Western and 'Islamic' World Views

1   Marks, J. and Cox, C., *Conflict or Concordat? A Comparison between Western Societies and Ideological Islamism*, in preparation; a shorter version of this pamphlet is being published as an Occasional Paper by the Centre for Islamic Studies, London Bible College.

2   Modernist Islam '...sought to reconcile Islamic faith and modern values such as constitutionalism, as well as cultural revival, nationalism, freedom of religious interpretation, scientific investigation, modern-style education, women's rights, and ... other themes ... this movement saw the tension between Islamic faith and modern values as a historical accident, not an inherent feature of Islam'; see Kurzman, C. (ed.), *Modernist Islam: A Sourcebook: 1840-1940*, Oxford University Press, 2002, pp. 4 *et seq*.

3   The themes discussed by the modernists have also been developed more recently by Muslim writers around the world; see Kurzman, C. (ed.), *Liberal Islam: A Sourcebook*, Oxford University Press, 1998.

4   For a comprehensive account of historical and modern developments in Islamic societies around the world see, Lapidus, I., *A History of Islamic Societies*, Cambridge University Press, 2002.

5   Ruthven, M., *Islam: A Very Short Introduction*, Oxford University Press, 1997, Chapter 1, pp. 1-8, gives a very helpful introduction to these distinctions.

6   *Nigerian Fact Finding Report*, Christian Solidarity Worldwide, 3-11 January, 2003.

7   See Chapters 2 and 3 below for a fuller analysis of the *shari'a*, the possible consequences of its implementation and the lack of independent sources of civil authority in Islamic political thought.

8   In particular it is the focus of the Hajj or pilgrimage to Mecca which all Muslims are required to make at some time; see Duran, K., *Children of Abraham: An Introduction to Islam for Jews*, The American Jewish Committee, 2001, pp. 189-91.

9   IICORR was launched in February, 2003; Caroline Cox is co-chairman of the organisation.

10   Weber, M., *The methodology of the social sciences*, tr. by Shils E. and Finch, H., The Free Press, 1949, pp. 89-95.

11   The term 'ideal' is not a value-based concept of ideal— 'perfect' or ultimately desirable—but refers to an abstract category at the level of 'ideas'.

12   For example on Nazi Germany see Johnson, P., *A History of the Modern World*, Weidenfeld and Nicolson, 1983; Davidowicz, L., *The War Against the Jews 1939-45*, Penguin, 1977; Brady, R.A., *The Spirit and Structure of German Fascism*, Gollancz, 1937; and Gilbert, M., *The Holocaust*, Collins, 1986; and on the former Soviet Union see Solzhenitsyn, A., *The Gulag Archipelago*, (3 Vol.), Fontana/Collins, 1974, 1976, 1978; Conquest, R., *The Great Terror*, Penguin, 1971, pp. 72-96; Sakharov, A., *My Country and the World*, Collins/Harvill, 1975; Schapiro, L., (1917), *The Russian Revolutions and the Origins of Present Day Communism*, Penguin, 1985; Kolakowski, L., *Main Currents of Marxism*, Oxford University Press, 1981; and Medvedev, Zh., *Soviet Science*, Oxford University Press, 1979 together with other sources in Marks, J., *Fried Snowballs: Communism in Theory and Practice*, The Claridge Press, 1990.

13   See, for example, Shultz, R.H. and Godson, R., *Dezinformatsia, Active Measures in Soviet Strategy*, Pergamon-Brassey, 1984; Mercer, P., *'Peace' of the Dead*, Policy Research Publications, 1986; and *The KGB Abroad: 'Active Measures' in Survey*, Vol. 27, No. 118/9, Autumn/Winter 1983, pp. 49-67 together with other sources in Jacka, K., Cox, C. and Marks, J., *Rape of Reason*, Churchill Press, 1975.

14   Podhoretz, N., 'Oslo: The Peacemongers Return' in *Commentary*, October, 2001, p. 23.

15 Hassan, N., 'An Arsenal of Believers: Talking to the "human bombs"', *New Yorker*, 19 November 2001; and the *Sunday Telegraph*, 9 December 2001; see also the detailed responses in the Arabic media in MEMRI (Middle East Media Research Institute) Report Nos 83 and 84, 12 and 13 February 2002.

16 In some ways the modern suicide bombers resemble the medieval Assassins or even the Kharijites who in the earliest years of Islam murdered a caliph—Ali, Mohammed's son-in-law—and justified it on religious grounds; see Lewis, B., *The Assassins: A Radical Sect in Islam*, Weidenfeld and Nicolson, 1967/2001, pp. x and 127.

2: Concepts of Knowledge and Truth

1 For an overview see Marks, J., *Science and the Making of the Modern World*, Heinemann, 1983 and the numerous references cited therein.

2 Popper, K., *Conjectures and Refutations*, Routledge and Kegan Paul, 1974; and *The Open Society and Its Enemies*, Routledge and Kegan Paul, 1966.

3 Grant, E., 'When did modern science begin?', *The American Scholar*, 66 (1997), pp. 105-13.

4 However in Islam such studies were frequently regarded as dangerous to the faith; see Huff, T., *The Rise of Early Modern Science: Islam, China and the West*, Cambridge University Press, 1993, pp. 153, 235.

5 It is worth noting that over these centuries Europe was in the period known as the Dark Ages during which much of the knowledge of the Ancient World had been lost.

6 Huff, T., *The Rise of Early Modern Science: Islam, China and the West*, Cambridge University Press, 1993, pp. 75, 153.

7 Lewis, B., *The Muslim Discovery of Europe*, New York and London: Norton and Co., 1982, pp. 229-30.

8   For further discussion see Lewis, B., *The Political Language of Islam*, The University of Chicago Press, 1988, p. 129, footnote 11.

9   The even more restrictive doctrines of al-Wahhab in eighteenth century Arabia also developed from the Hanbali school and have spread world wide in the twentieth and twenty-first centuries following their espousal by the royal family of Saudi Arabia; see Algar, H., *Wahhabism: A Critical Essay*, Islamic Publications International, 2002.

10 See in particular Chapter 2, 'Knowledge and Truth', pp. 19-41 and Chapter 6, 'Education', pp. 123-35 in Marks, J., *Fried Snowballs: Communism in Theory and Practice*, The Claridge Press, 1990.

11 All dates are AD or CE. Muslims date their years from 622 AD—the date of Mohammed's migration or *hijra* from Mecca to Medina. The Muslim year is based on lunar months and is about 11 days shorter than the calendar or solar year used in the West; this means that the regular annual Muslim festivals such as the fast in the month of Ramadan occur on a different date each year on the Western calendar.

12 Rippin, A., *Muslims: Their Religious Beliefs and Practices*, Routledge, 2001, p. 46.

13 This did not prevent the inclusion of 'Western' subjects such as science, engineering, technology and medicine in some schools and colleges in the Muslim world, for example in the Ottoman empire, Egypt and India in the nineteenth century and more widely across the Muslim world in the twentieth century.

14 This does not mean that the *'ulema'*, individually and collectively, do not argue, reason and dispute about truth and their methodology for finding it as their extensive writings over the centuries show; the fundamental difference remains that Western academics make use of much wider categories of evidence, subject matter and styles of reasoning as we have tried to indicate in the text and in Table 1 (p. 27).

15 See, for example, the curriculum of the influential Al-Azhar University in Cairo; it was only in 1961 that Al-Azhar was transformed into a partly secular university and began to offer courses in the sciences and engineering—see the Al-Azhar website and Sivan, E. *Radical Islam: Medieval Theology and Modern Politics*, Yale University Press, 1990, p. 51.

16 See, for example:

> ...the Quran is unique among sacred scriptures in teaching a doctrine of abrogation according to which later pronouncements of the Prophet abrogate, i.e. declare null and void, his earlier pronouncements. The importance of knowing which verses abrogate others has given rise to the Quranic science known as *Nasikh wa Mansukh* i.e. 'the Abrogators and the Abrogated'. [Jeffery, A., *Islam: Muhammad and his Religion*, Bobbs Merrill, 1958, p. 66.]

For further detailed discussion and many sources see, Masood, S., *Naskh: Al-Nasikh wa al-Mansukh - A study of the Islamic theory of abrogation, its formulation, development and use today*, Thesis for Master of Theology, London Bible College, Brunel University, March 2001; see, in particular, pp. 9-11, 22-24. For lists of books on *naskh* see, Zaid, M., *al- Naskh fi al-Quran al-Karim*, Dar al-Fikr, Cairo, 1963, Vol. 1, pp. 290-395. All four major schools of law recognise the concept of abrogation although they differ in the details of its application; see Ibn al-Arabi, *alNasikh wa al-Mansukh fi al-Quran al-Karim*, Dar al-Kutub, Beirut, 1997, pp. 12-13. Like many other topics concerning Islam there are numerous relatively minor differences of meaning and interpretation amongst Islamic scholars over the centuries.

17 Gabriel, M., *Islam and Terrorism*, Charisma House, 2002, pp. 31-32; verses from the Koran are, unless otherwise stated, taken from *The Holy Qur'an*, translation and commentary by Abdullah Yusuf Ali, IPCI—Islamic Vision, 1934 and 1999.

18 Huff, T., *The Rise of Early Modern Science: Islam, China and the West*, Cambridge University Press, 1993, p. 214.

19 Lewis, B., *The Assassins: A Radical Sect in Islam*, Weidenfeld and Nicolson, 1967/2001, p. 126.

20 For an outline of later developments and complexities see Lewis, B. (ed.), *The World of Islam: Faith, People, Culture*, Thames and Hudson, 1992, 'Outline of Islamic History', p. 10 and 'Chronological Chart of Islam', p. 348.

21 Lewis, B., *Islam and the West*, Oxford University Press, 1993, pp. 129, 130.

22 The question of sources is clearly and briefly discussed in Cook, M., *Muhammad*, Oxford University Press, 1983, Chapter 7, pp. 61-76.

23 Warraq, I., *Why I am Not a Muslim*, Prometheus Books, 1995; *The Quest for the Historical Muhammad*, Prometheus Books, 2000; *What the Koran Really Says*, Prometheus Books, 2002; Rippin, A., *Literary Analysis of Koran, Tafsir, and Sira: The Methodologies of John Wansbrough*, in Warraq, I. (ed.), *The Origins of the Koran: Classic Essays on Islam's Holy Book*, Prometheus Books, 1998; Wansbrough, J., *The Sectarian Milieu: Content and Composition of Islamic Salvation History*, Oxford University Press, 1978; Crone, P. and Cook, M., *Hagarism: The Making of the Muslim World*, Cambridge University Press, 1977; Crone, P., *Slaves on Horses: The Evolution of the Islamic Polity*, Cambridge University Press, 1980; Crone, P., *Meccan Trade and the Rise of Islam*, Princeton University Press, 1987.

24 Wansbrough, J., *Quranic Studies: sources and methods of scriptural interpretation*, Oxford University Press, 1977, p. ix, Preface.

25 Rippin, A., *Muslims: Their Religious Beliefs and Practices*, Vol. 1, London, 1991, p. ix, Preface; see also Rippin, A., *Literary Analysis of Koran, Tafsir, and Sira: The Methodologies of John Wansbrough*, in Warraq, I. (ed.), *The Origins of the Koran: Classic Essays on*

Islam's Holy Book, Prometheus Books, 1998,
pp. 354, 358.

26 Rippin, *Literary Analysis of Koran, Tafsir, and Sira:
The Methodologies of John Wansbrough* 1998, pp. 354,
358.

27 Sakharov, A., *My Country and the World*,
Collins/Harvill, 1975, p. 31.

28 The list would also include the dynamics and optics of
Galileo and Newton, the flowering of the mathematical
and the experimental sciences during the eighteenth
century Enlightenment, the chemical revolution of
Lavoisier and Mendeleev and the emergence of biology
and geology in the nineteenth century in the work of
men such as Lyell, Linnaeus, Darwin and Mendel.

29 Gutas, D., *Greek Thought, Arabic Culture: The Graeco-
Arabic Translation Movement in Baghdad and Early
Abbasid Society*, Routledge, 1998.

30 Habgood, J., *Varieties of Unbelief*, Darton Longman
and Todd, 2000, pp. 77-79.

31 Akbar S. Ahmed, *Postmodernism and Islam*, Routledge,
1992, p. 93. Italics added.

3: Political and Social Structures

1 For example on Nazi Germany see Johnson, P., *A
History of the Modern World*, Weidenfeld and Nicolson,
1983; Davidowicz, L., *The War Against the Jews 1939-
45*, Penguin, 1977; Brady, R.A., *The Spirit and
Structure of German Fascism*, Gollancz, 1937; and
Gilbert, M., *The Holocaust*, Collins, 1986; and on the
former Soviet Union see Solzhenitsyn, A., *The Gulag
Archipelago*, (3 Vol.), Fontana/Collins, 1974, 1976,
1978; Conquest, R., *The Great Terror*, Penguin, 1971,
pp. 72-96; Sakharov, A., *My Country and the World*,
Collins/Harvill, 1975; Schapiro, L., (1917), *The Russian
Revolutions and the Origins of Present Day
Communism*, Penguin, 1985; Kolakowski, L., *Main
Currents of Marxism*, Oxford University Press, 1981;
and Medvedev, Zh., *Soviet Science*, Oxford University
Press, 1979 together with other sources in Marks, J.,

Fried Snowballs: Communism in Theory and Practice,
The Claridge Press, 1990.

2   As we have mentioned (see p. 3), some Muslims are
currently attempting to embrace change within an
Islamic system; however these attempts are relatively
recent, are often based in the West and seem to have
little momentum or credence in the Islamic countries.

3   St Matthew's Gospel, Ch 22, v 15-22.

4   Lewis, B., *The Political Language of Islam,* The
University of Chicago Press, 1988, p. 72.

5   Kramer, M., 'Islam vs Democracy', in *Commentary,*
January 1993, p. 38.

6   Lewis, B., *The Political Language of Islam,* The
University of Chicago Press, 1988, pp. 72-73; for
further elaboration see pp. 77-8. See the *Appendix -
Contemporary Case Studies* for contemporary accounts
of *jihad* in Sudan, Nigeria and Indonesia. In Sudan, a
report in January 2003 showed a recognition that the
National Islamic Front government are themselves
publicly proclaiming that the violent conflict there is a
jihad.

7   Lewis, *The Political Language of Islam,* pp. 84-85; see
the *Appendix - Contemporary Case Studies* for a
contemporary account of this practice in Indonesia.

8   Surah 101:6-9, (Mecca), *The Holy Qur'an.*

9   Surahs 8:39, 4:74 and 9:89, (All Medina).

10 See the way in which Osama bin Laden uses the
concepts of *jihad* and paradise in his declaration of war
on America:

> ... a martyr's privileges are guaranteed by Allah;
> forgiveness with the first gush of his blood, he will be
> shown his seat in paradise, he will be decorated with
> the jewels of Imaan [belief], married off to the
> beautiful ones, protected from the test in the grave,
> assured security in the day of judgement, crowned
> with the crown of dignity, a ruby of which is better
> than Duniah [the whole world] and its entire content,
> wedded to seventy two of the pure Houries [beautiful

ones of paradise], and his intercession on behalf of seventy of his relatives will be accepted.

Extract from the Declaration of War by Osama bin Laden, together with leaders of the World Islamic Front for the *jihad* Against the Jews and the Crusaders [Al-Jabhah al-Islamiyyah al-'Alamiyyah Li-Qital al-Yahud Wal-Salibiyyin], Afghanistan, February 23, 1998; quoted in Gunaratna, R., *Inside Al Qaeda: Global Network of Terror*, London: Hurst and Company, 2002, pp. 1, 7.

11 Gabriel, M., *Islam and Terrorism*, Charisma House, 2002, p. 31.

12 See surahs 2:217; 4:71-104; 8:24-36 and 39-65. (All Medina.)

13 See also surahs 47:4, 9:123, 8:67, 8:59-60. (All Medina.)

14 For a graphic overview see Fregosi, P., *Jihad in the West: Muslim Conquests from the 7th to the 21st Centuries*, Prometheus Books, 1998; for more detail see Holt, P., Lambton, A. and Lewis, B. (eds), *The Cambridge History of Islam*, Cambridge University Press, 1970.

15 Lewis, B., *Cultures in Conflict: Christians, Muslims, and Jews in the Age of Discovery*, Oxford University Press, 1995, pp. 11-12.

16 For example the brutalities perpetrated by Crusaders when they took Jerusalem in the twelfth century and those by Muslims when they captured Contantinople in 1453.

17 Mayer, A., *Islam and Human Rights: Tradition and Politics*, Westview Press/Pinter Publishers, 1991.

18 Mayer, *Islam and Human Rights: Tradition and Politics*, p. 91.

19 Mayer, *Islam and Human Rights: Tradition and Politics*, pp. 186-87.

20 For more detail see Gabriel, *Islam and Terrorism*, 2002, pp. 42-43.

21 Gabriel, *Islam and Terrorism*, 2002, pp. 42-43.

22 Mayer, *Islam and Human Rights: Tradition and Politics*, 1991, p. 136. We recognise that while modern Western societies have considerably advanced women's rights and opportunities, they also allow many undesirable features—loss of dignity, promiscuity, pornography—which are deplored by many Muslims, even those who would not accept the traditional Islamic restrictions on women or who argue that traditional Islam provided more rights for women than other societies at that time or earlier.

23 Bat Ye'or, *The Dhimmi: Jews and Christians under Islam*, Associated University Press, 1985; *The Decline of Eastern Christianity*, Associated University Presses, 1996; *Islam and Dhimmitude: Where Civilisations Collide*, Associated University Presses, 2002. We recognise that when *dhimmi* status was first introduced it provided more rights for Christians and Jews under Muslim rule than Christian societies, either then or later, gave to Muslims or Jews.

24 Mayer, *Islam and Human Rights: Tradition and Politics*, 1991, p. 160.

25 See Lewis, B., *Race and Slavery in the Middle East: An Historical Enquiry*, New York and Oxford: Oxford University Press, 1990; Lovejoy, P., *Transformations in Slavery: A history of slavery in Africa*, Cambridge University Press, 1983; Marmon, S. (ed.), *Slavery in the Islamic Middle East*, Markus Wiener (Princeton), 1999; Crone, P., *Slaves on Horses: The Evolution of the Islamic Polity*, Cambridge University Press, 1980.

26 See the *Appendix - Contemporary Case Studies* for a contemporary account of slavery in Sudan.

27 Pipes, D., *Slave Soldiers and Islam: The Genesis of a Military System*, Yale University Press, 1981, p. 45.

28 Azumah, J., *Islam and Slavery*, Centre for Islamic Studies, London Bible College, 1999, p. 3. See also Azumah, J., *The Legacy of Arab-Islam in Africa*, Oneworld Publications, 2001 for a comprehensive and detailed account of slavery and Islam in Africa, including a discussion of the role of *shari'a* and *jihad*, from pre-colonial times to the present.

29 Gordon, M., *Slavery in the Arab World*, New Amsterdam Books, 1987, p. ix. The Atlantic slave trade was important from about 1650 to 1850 and peaked just before 1800, whereas the intra-African slave trade started earlier and went on later; its most important years were from 1750 to 1900, with a peak around 1850; see Manning, P., *Slavery and African life: Occidental, Oriental and African Slave Trades*, Cambridge University Press, 1990, pp. 9-12.

30 For a comprehensive account see Thomas, H., *The Slave Trade: The History of the Atlantic Slave Trade 1440-1870*, Simon and Schuster, 1997, see also the many references cited therein.

31 Azumah, *Islam and Slavery*, 1999, p. 5.

32 House of Lords Hansard, col. 333-356, 14 July 1960.

33 Note presented by the Secretary-General to the 50th Session of the United Nations General Assembly, 16 October 1995.

34 Lovejoy, P. and Hogendoorn, J. (eds), *Slow Death for Slavery: The Course of Abolition in Northern Nigeria, 1897-1936*, Cambridge University Press, 1993, p. 30.

35 Gordon, M., *Slavery in the Arab World*, New Amsterdam Books, 1987/1992; Introduction to the American Edition; see also Segal, R., *Islam's Black Slaves: The other black diaspora*, Farrar, Straus and Giroux, 2001; and Manning, P., *Slavery and African Life: Occidental, Oriental, and African Slave Trades*, Cambridge University Press, 1990.

36 Lewis, B., *Cultures in Conflict: Christians, Muslims, and Jews in the Age of Discovery*, OUP, 1995, p. 72.

37 MEMRI website on www.memri.org/

38 See Lewis, B. (ed.), *Islam from the Prophet Muhammad to the Capture of Constantinople*; Vol. II *Religion and Society*, Oxford University Press, 1987, pp. 124-25.

39 2001 World Development Indicators database, World Bank; it makes very little difference to the argument if the data are expressed in $US or International dollars with purchasing power parity.

40 *Arab Human Development Report 2002: Overview - A future for all*, United Nations Development Programme, 2002, p. 2.

41 *Arab Human Development Report 2002: Overview - A future for all*, 2002, p. 3.

42 *Arab Human Development Report 2002: Overview - A future for all*, 2002, p. 8.

43 *Arab Human Development Report 2002: Overview - A future for all*, 2002, p. 9.

44 Huff, T., *The Rise of Early Modern Science: Islam, China and the West*, Cambridge: Cambridge University Press, 1993, p. 2.

45 Makdisi, A., *The Rise of Colleges, Institutions of Learning in Islam and the West*, Edinburgh University Press, 1981, p. 78.

46 Huff, *The Rise of Early Modern Science: Islam, China and the West*, 1993, p. 153.

47 More recently *madrasas* also include schools.

48 Huff, *The Rise of Early Modern Science: Islam, China and the West*, 1993, p. 2.

49 Sabra, A., 'Situating Arabic science: locality versus essence', *Isis*, 87, 1996, pp. 654-69.

50 See Huff, *The Rise of Early Modern Science: Islam, China and the West*, 1993, p. 83, FN 128; Shaw, S., *History of the Ottoman Empire and Modern Turkey*, New York: Cambridge University Press, 1976, 1: pp. 235-38. It is interesting to note that a captured (and converted) Hungarian Calvinist (or Unitarian) was responsible for introducing the printing press to the Muslim community in Turkey early in the eighteenth century; *ibid.*, p. 236.

51 Lewis, B., *The Muslim Discovery of Europe*, Norton, 1982; extracts from pp. 223-24.

52 Hussaini, S., 'Toward the rebirth and development of Shariyyah science and technology', *MAAS Journal of Islamic Science* 1, No. 2, 1985, pp. 81-94; at p. 83.

53 As cited in Hoodbhoy, P., *Islam and Science: Religious Orthodoxy and the Battle for Rationality*, with a foreword by Mohammed Abdus Salam, London: Zed Books Ltd, 1990, p. 28.

54 Hussaini, 'Toward the rebirth and development of Shariyya science and technology', p. 83.

55 Huff, *The Rise of Early Modern Science: Islam, China and the West*, 1993, p. 235.

56 Another factor may have been the hostility shown by Islamists in Pakistan to the Ahmadi sect to which Salam belongs culminating in its designation as non-Islamic in 1974; see Nasr, S., *Islamic Leviathan*, Oxford, 2001, p. 98.

4: Conflicts between Western and Islamic Societies

1 This chapter can only outline these themes and give some indicative examples as evidence: for more detail see Marks J. and Cox, C., *Conflict or Concordat?: A Comparison between Western Societies and Ideological Islamism*, forthcoming.

2 For further information and discussion see 'Islam is the Power of the Future', Chapter 9 in Kramer, M., *Arab Awakening and Islamic Revival: The Politics of Ideas in the Middle East*, Transaction Publishers, 1996, pp. 141-59.

3 Kramer, *Arab Awakening and Islamic Revival*, 1996, p. 143.

4 Kramer, *Arab Awakening and Islamic Revival*, 1996, p. 148.

5 Mawdudi, M., *Jihad in Islam*, India, 1970s; quoted in Gabriel, M., *Islam and Terrorism*, Charisma House, 2002, p. 82.

6 For more information on Banna and the Muslim Brotherhood see Lia, B., *The Society of the Muslim Brothers in Egypt: The Rise of an Islamic Mass Movement 1928-1942*, Ithaca Press, 1998; and Mitchell, R., *The Society of the Muslim Brothers*, Oxford University Press, 1993.

7   www.ummah.org.uk/ikhwan/; the site carries this
    extraordinary disclaimer (spelling as in original):
    Important Disclaimer: The maintainer of this page is
    not a member of Al-Ikhwan party and does not approve
    or agree with everything they say. This page is there
    for the soul perpose of answering the questions you
    always had and never knew who to ask. This page has
    no political perpose of any kind and no connection
    whatsoever to any organization or institution.

8   In addition, Qutb has written extensively on many
    aspects of Islam; see, for example Qutb, S., *Social
    Justice in Islam*, (trans. J. B. Hardie), New York:
    Islamic Publications International, 2000, and the
    bibliography on p. 325.

9   Kramer, M., *Arab Awakening and Islamic Revival: The
    Politics of Ideas in the Middle East*, Transaction
    Publishers, 1996, pp. 148-49.

10 Qutb, S., 'Signs along the road', quoted in Hammoda,
    A., *Sayyid Qutb: From the Village to the Gallows*, Cairo:
    Sinai Publishing, 1987.

11 Jansen, J., *The Dual Nature of Islamic Funda-
    mentalism*, London: Hurst and Co, 1997, p. 180.

12 Kramer, M., 'Islam vs Democracy', in *Commentary*,
    January 1993, pp. 38-39.

13 Warburg, G., 'Turabi of the Sudan: Soft-spoken
    Revolutionary', in Kramer, M. (ed.), *Middle Eastern
    Lectures: Number One*, The Moshe Dayan Centre for
    Middle Eastern and African Studies, 1995, pp. 85-97;
    Miller, J., 'The Charismatic Islamists', in Kramer, M.
    (ed.), *Middle Eastern Lectures: Number Two*, The
    Moshe Dayan Center for Middle Eastern and African
    Studies, Tel Aviv University, 1997, pp. 39-46; El-
    Affendi, A., *Turabi's Revolution: Islam and Power in
    Sudan and Who Needs an Islamic State*, Grey Seal
    Publications, 1991; Hamdi, M., *The Making of an
    Islamic Political Leader: Coversations with Hasan al-
    Turabi*, Westview Press, 1998.

14 Duran, K., *Children of Abraham: An Introduction to Islam for Jews*, American Jewish Committee, 2001, pp. 136-37.

15 Bodansky, Y., *Bin Laden: The Man Who Declared War on America*, Forum, Prima Publishing, 1999; Alexander, Y. and Swetnam, M., *Usama Bin Laden's al-Qaida: Profile of a Terrorist Network*, Transnational Publishers, February, 2001.

16 Halliday, F., *Two Hours that Shook the World, September 11, 2001: Causes and Consequences*, Saqi Books, 2002, Appendix 1.

17 Kramer, 'Islam vs Democracy', 1993, pp. 38-39.

18 Kramer, 'Islam is the Power of the Future', Chapter 9, in Kramer, M., *Arab Awakening and Islamic Revival*, Transaction Publishers, 1996, p. 142.

19 Murad, K., *The Islamic Movement in the West: Reflections on Some Issues*, The Islamic Foundation, 1981; (Addresses given as The Islamic Foundation, 233 London Road, Leicester LE2 1ZE, United Kingdom; Quran House, PO Box 30611, Nairobi, Kenya; and P.M.B. 3193, Kano, Nigeria).

20 Murad, *The Islamic Movement in the West*, 1981, p. 3.

21 The verses quoted are Sura 9.19-21, 40: Sura 48.28: Sura 2.216 (All Medina).

22 Report in the San Ramon Valley Herald of a speech to California Muslims in July 1998; quoted by Pipes, D., in 'CAIR: Moderate Friends of Terror', *New York Post*, 22 April 2002.

23 Kramer, 'Islam vs Democracy', 1993, p. 38.

24 Whine, M., *Cyberspace - a New Medium for Communication, Command and Control by Extremists in Studies in Conflict and Terrorism*, Rand, May 1999; Whine, M., *Islamist Organisations on the Internet*, International Centre for Terrorism, April 1998.

25 See Whine, *Cyberspace - The New Medium for Communication, Command and Control by Extremist*, 1999, p. 8.

26 Al-Muhajiroun Meeting at Friends Meeting House, Euston Road, Friday 12 November 1999.

27 It was extraordinarily ironic and profoundly disturbing to hear these exhortations to systematic and world-wide violence in the Friends Meeting House which has been the London headquarters of the pacifist Quakers for so many years.

28 Demonstration on Friday 17 March 2000, 3.30-5.30 pm; conference on Saturday 18 March, 2000 at 6.00 pm.

29 Amnesty International, 17 October 1994; reported on MSA news.

30 FAS Intelligence Resource Program at www.fas.org/irp/world/ara/ladin.tym

31 Whine, M., *Islamist Organisations on the Internet*, International Centre for Terrorism, April 1998 on www.ict.org

32 See *Extremism and intolerance on campus*, CVCP, July 1998 and Anthony McRoy, PhD Thesis. McRoy argues that it would be better to allow radical Islamists to organise on campuses and to oppose their arguments in open debate; he contends that the present implicit ban on Islamist organisations is seen by many young Muslims as evidence of explicit prejudice against the whole of Islam.

33 Rashid, A., *Jihad: The Rise of Militant Islam in Central Asia*, Yale University Press, 2002.

34 See 'Islamic *Jihad* Groups'; supplement in *Republika*, Jakarta, 1 June 2002.

35 See autopost@mail.nahdah.org

36 Speech by Baroness Cox in the debate on the Queen's Speech, House of Lords Hansard, 14 November 2002.

37 Bakewell, J., 'The believers who despise our ways', *New Statesman*, 29 May 29 and 'Correspondent' on BBC2, 3 June 2000.

38 www.tanzeem.org

39 See zagh@aol

40 www.debate.org.uk; and www. answering-islam.org

41 http://main.faithfreedom.org/; and http://www.secularislam.org/

42 These further links can be found, respectively, on http://main.faithfreedom.org/links.htm and on http://www.secularislam.org/links/index.htm and http://www.geocities.com/ListIslam/

43 Riddell, P., 'Saddam and Deception', *LBC Centre for Islamic Studies Newsletter*, Winter 1998-9, pp. 2-3.

44 See also 'The Islamic agenda and its blueprints' in *Evangelicals Now*, March 2002 which quotes a *hadith* thus:

> ...to lie is one of the major sins and Allah will hold you accountable, with the exception of these three (in other words, in these three situations you can lie as much as you need to...): (1) With your women. (2) In espionage *jihad* when you are a minority. and (3) in maintaining peace.

45 *Islamophobia - A Challenge For Us All*, Report of the Runnymede Trust Commission on British Muslims and Islamophobia, The Runnymede Trust, 1997; this report was launched by Jack Straw when he was Home Secretary.

46 *Addressing the Challenge of Islamophobia*, The Runnymede Trust, 2001; although this report was published after September 11, it apparently makes no reference to the attack on the twin towers of the World Trade Centre.

47 *The Westophobia Report: Anti-Western and Anti-Christian Stereotyping in British Muslim Publications*, Centre for Islamic Studies, London Bible College, 1999.

48 *The Westophobia Report,*1999, p. 14.

49 *Anti-Muslim Discrimination and Hostility in the United Kingdom, 2000*, Islamic Human Rights Commission.

50 At a meeting at the House of Lords on Wednesday, 16 February 2000, chaired by Lord Ahmed of Rotherham and attended by Home Office Minister, Mike O'Brien.

51 The IHRC has, according to its website (www.ihrc.org), also been involved in a number of other publications and campaigns concerning Islamic issues around the world—for example in Iraq, the Sudan, Uzbekistan, Chechnya, Lebanon, Turkey, Nigeria, Palestine, South Africa, India, Bosnia and Kosovo.

52 Speech by Baroness Cox in the debate on the Queen's Speech, House of Lords Hansard, 14 November 2002.

53 'Attorney John Loftus launches lawsuit exposing US Federal cover-up of Saudi Florida terror ring', in *Root and Branch Association Islam-Israeli Fellowship News Digest*, 16 May 2002, pp. 3-32; available from rb@rb.org.il

54 WAMY's website claims that: 'WAMY is the first International Islamic Organization dealing specially with youth affairs embracing over 450 Islamic youth / students organization in the five continents.'

55 *Islamic Extremism: A Viable Threat to U.S. National Security*, An Open Forum at the U.S. Department of State, 7 January 1999, Transcript of Presentation by Shaykh Mohammed Hisham Kabbani; see also an interview with Shaykh Kabbani in *Middle East Quarterly*, June, 2000.

56 Emerson, S., *American Jihad: The Terrorists Living Amongst Us*, The Free Press, 2002.

5: Challenges to Western Societies

1   Fisk, R., 'Remember the First Holocaust', *Independent*, Friday, 28 January 2000.

2   Ahmed, A.S., *Postmodernism and Islam: Predicament and Promise*, Routledge, 1992, pp. 168-69; Said, E., 'Arabesque', in *New Statesman*, 7 September 1990, p. 31.

3   The preservation and transmission of their own culture should be a voluntary and private activity as it has been, both historically and currently, for numerous other cultural minorities in Western societies.

6: The Challenge to Islam

1   Duran, K., *Children of Abraham: An Introduction to Islam for Jews*, American Jewish Committee, 2001, pp. 260, 262.

2   Ali, T., *The Clash of Fundamentalisms: Crusades, Jihads and Modernity*, Verso, 2002, pp. 312-13.

3   Ahmed, A.S., *Postmodernism and Islam*, Routledge, 1992, p. 93. Italics added.

4   Jaki, S.L., *Science and Creation*, Scottish Academic Press, 1986, p. 210.

5   Habgood, J., *Varieties of Unbelief*, Darton Longman and Todd, 2000, pp. 77-79.

Appendix

1   For a comprehensive account see Thomas, H., *The Slave Trade: The History of the Atlantic Slave Trade 1440-1870*, Simon and Schuster, 1997; see also the many references cited therein.

2   Azumah, J., *The Legacy of Arab-Islam in Africa*, Oneworld Publications, 2001.

3   Names not provided in case of capture and reprisal.

4   Nazer, M. with Lewis, D., *Sklavin*, Schneekluth, 2002 (in German); *Slave*, Doubleday, 2003, forthcoming (in English).

5   This was verified by the surgeon in our group.